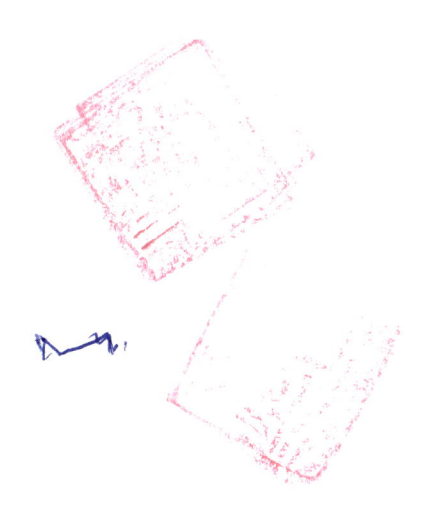

From a Hotelier to Parkinson's Disease

FROM A HOTELIER TO PARKINSON'S DISEASE

Tony Burrows

Copyright © 2014 by Tony Burrows.

All rights reserved. No part of this publication may be reproduced, distributed, or transmitted in any form or by any means, including photocopying, recording, or other electronic or mechanical methods, without the prior written permission of the publisher, except in the case of brief quotations embodied in critical reviews and certain other noncommercial uses permitted by copyright law. For permission requests, write to the publisher, addressed "Attention: Permissions Coordinator," at the address below.

BookVenture Publishing LLC
1000 Country Lane Ste 300
Ishpeming MI 49849
www.bookventure.com
Hotline: 1(877) 276-9751
Fax: 1(877) 864-1686

Ordering Information:
Quantity sales. Special discounts are available on quantity purchases by corporations, associations, and others. For details, contact the publisher at the address above.

Printed in the United States of America

Library of Congress Control Number:	2014949110
ISBN-13: Softcover	978-1-941736-16-6
Pdf	978-1-941736-17-3
ePub	978-1-941736-18-0
Kindle	978-1-941736-19-7

Rev. date: 11/11/2014

Disclaimer

This publication is designed to provide accurate and personal experience information in regard to the subject matter covered. It is sold with the understanding that the author, contributors, publisher are not engaged in rendering counseling or other professional services. If counseling advice or other expert assistance is required, the services of a competent professional person should be sought out.

* * *

This book is dedicated to my wife, Morni, my eldest son Chris, my daughter Michelle, my youngest son Daniel, and my good friends Eamonn Sadler and Erik Rufer, without whose love and support, would not have allowed me to write this book, whilst experiencing my present *condition*.

My purpose of writing this book (and subsequent others that will follow) is because, since being stricken with this degenerative "neurological nightmare," am pretty much unable to communicate verbally and had lost any handwriting skill almost two years ago; and so I felt the need to put my "finger to the keyboard" only to be able to describe to my kids (and subsequent grandchildren) what had happened, in their younger days, to their dad (and grandpop) after having been through an extremely bitter and heartrending divorce.

My name is Tony Burrows and on March 26 of 2012, I was diagnosed as having Parkinson's disease.

* * *

CONTENTS

Chapter One:	The Worst Day of My Life (A True Story, As Best As I Can Recall)	9
Chapter Two:	Where It Had All Begun Twenty-Seven Years Earlier	20
Chapter Three:	Switzerland Here We Come	26
Chapter Four:	My First Day in the "Real World"	35
Chapter Five:	"D" Day	41
Chapter Six:	The Hills are Alive, With the Sound of Music?	47
Chapter Seven:	Homeward Bound	54
Chapter Eight:	Back to Square One	56
Chapter 9:	The Day the World Lost Barry Earl	61
Chapter Ten:	The Worst Shift You Could Ask a Man to Cover	67
Chapter Eleven:	Off to the Sane Part of the World?	77
Chapter Twelve:	A Month in Spain	84
Chapter Thirteen:	It's Off to Good Old Blighty	90
Chapter Fourteen:	London Here We Come	94
Chapter Fifteen:	Oh Canada, Our Home and Native Land	104
Chapter Sixteen:	We Had Arrived at Our New Home	117
Chapter Seventeen:	Southeast Asia (Part 1)	125
Chapter Eighteen:	Enter the Big "C"	136
Chapter Nineteen:	Back to Our Home Vancouver	145
Chapter Twenty:	Southeast Asia (Part 2)	151
Chapter Twenty-One:	Please, Not India!	160
Chapter Twenty-Two:	India Here We Come (Heaven Help Us)!	166
Chapter Twenty-Three:	Fiji Here We Come	173
Chapter Twenty-Four:	Out From Thy Frying Pan and Into the Fire!	186
Chapter Twenty-Five:	Vancouver, Here We Come, Again!	197
Chapter Twenty-Six:	It Was San Francisco Time	201
Chapter Twenty-Seven:	A New String to My Bow (So As to Speak)	212
Chapter Twenty-Eight:	The Unadulterated "Journeys"	223

CHAPTER ONE

The Worst Day of My Life
(A True Story, As Best As I Can Recall)

IT WAS 2:30 A.M. WHEN the phone rang. I knew I was on the emergency shift at 3:30 a.m. based on our crisis meeting the day before. It was Jean Louis Ripoche, our general manager, who said to me, "Look out of your window!" As I got out of bed, I wondered why he had asked me to do such a thing.

I was part of the executive committee of Le Meridien Hotel that had been entrusted to protect our "home" from a potentially ensuing attack by the rioters that had taken the city by storm.

We had just a couple of hours previous to this, been to each and every room, unscrewing each light bulb in the event that, should our hotel be attacked, they would assume it was vacant and that nobody was in house.

We were in Jakarta, Indonesia, back in 1988, when the people had decided to revolt against the government, run by Soeharto and his family, for the increase of fuel prices as well as the deflation of the Rupiah against the U.S. dollar. (It had risen from Rp 2,150 to an astonishing Rp 15,000 to each U.S. dollar) This meant that my salary had increased from a U.S. dollar value of $3,800 (tax-free, live in) to an approximate value of $26,511 per month or $318,138 per year!

Our hotel was owned by the half-brother of President Soeharto, and so being guilty by association was, in essence, the reason we were the target of the anger that pursued.

My wife now, or fiancée then, had just been chaperoned to the airport because she looked Chinese (at this point in time the Chinese held seventy two percent of the wealth in Jakarta and represented five percent of the entire population and were despised by the Muslims). We had driven her in an unmarked hotel car, with two gun-wielding security guards, to the airport for her safe exit from the city, to her Mum and Dad's residence on the island of Borneo. It was the trip back from the airport that I witnessed something that cut me the core. I had no idea that the Chinese were hated so much until, as we approached a check point, I saw this middle-aged Chinese chap, getting dragged from his Mercedes Benz by a bunch of antigovernment activists, and was literally shot in the head—execution style. I vomited into my lap and shouted to our driver to "stop," only to be reminded that I was foreigner and that I would be endangering myself for what would have been a futile attempt at demanding some sort of justice. "Pak Tony, please keep your head down low." It would have appeared anybody who had a few bucks in their pocket were fair game.

Having listened to my boss, I looked out of my bedroom window that faced Jalan Sudirman, one of the main artery roads that stretched from the heart of the city, to the main toll road that would take you to the airport. What I saw brought a chill to my spine.

The one hundred and seventy-five heavily armed army personnel that had been hired by the hotel owner to protect his hotel from an impending attack, were in fact, so scared of the potential outcome of the attack and had decided to run for their lives, leaving us helpless. I could see them scurrying in the darkness. Word had got out that the 150,000 antigovernment extremists were heading down Jalan Sudirman from a place called Senin, that was approximately five miles away but on the west side of the highway (we were on the east).

Earlier in the day, we had decided that our best defense would be to have all the fire hoses positioned so that they faced the hotel entrance. A few days prior to this, we had barricaded the hotel entrance up like wooden fortresses as they had been demonstrating outside our hotel and had hurled large rocks at us as we watched from inside the lobby.

The phone rang again as I was exiting the shower after what seemed to a minute under cold water. It was Jean Louis again saying, "Meeting in the lobby now." There was an air of authority in his voice with a slight tremor.

He was going to have to lead us through this crisis no matter what.

We had been in touch with head office earlier in the day and had been advised to leave the hotel just as soon as we had a chance. We (all six of us expats) had all packed an overnight bag and had stored it in the GM's suite without the local staff knowing. If they had found out that we had planned to fly out that afternoon by helicopter, they would quite possibly have organized a lynch mob. As it happened, the helicopter did not arrive as the city was filled with acrid smoke from all the buildings and cars the rioters had set ablaze and so the pilot had deemed it unsafe to even attempt to land on the hotel helipad.

We met in the lobby, all very quiet as the GM went over the escape route we had mapped out at 5:00 p.m. the previous afternoon, in the event the fire hoses did not have the desired effect.

There was myself, the GM, and our financial controller by the name of Netraj (a native of Mauritius) manning the hoses and the front office manager (Dominique), another Canadian such as myself; the executive chef (Antoine), a native from France; and Michael Allen, our Australian director of sales and marketing—all ready at the valves awaiting the GM's order to turn them on.

And we waited in absolute silence. Until today, I have never felt so helplessly vulnerable and lonely as I did, at this point, in my life.

We all took our positions and again waited in absolute silence.

We had turned off our flashlights so we're now in pitch darkness. I could hear Netraj's breath as he sucked in hard. I whispered to him, "Are you okay?" But he couldn't speak through fear. I said to him, "Because I'm not." I was hoping this would put his mind at ease even if only a little. No reply was heard.

It was the GM who said, "Listen!" We could now hear the ruckus from within the hotel, which meant they were getting closer. Then it started, the familiar noise we had heard only two days prior. The gunshots. I gripped my fire hose with relentless abandon expecting the noise to get closer and louder until they were coming at the hotel entrance.

But it didn't. The shots were real and the noise was real but it wasn't getting any closer. The GM's cell phone went off and it was Patrice, the GM of the Holiday Inn that was at the crossroads to the highway and Jalan Sudirman—and the news was good. The rioters were being headed off by a barrage of riot police that had just appeared out of nowhere, along with some tanks and armored vehicles that had rolled in from within the dense brush that surrounded the Hilton Hotel. We, all six of us, just placed our hoses on the ground, moved away from the water valves and wept with joy and hugged each other as the pending and almost certain disaster had been avoided.

That same day, both Netraj and I were informed we would be leaving for Singapore. *Hallelujah*, I thought to myself, but then a wave of disappointment came over me as upon checking my passport, I realized I did not have a valid exit visa! It had expired one week earlier. So what was I to do? There was only one thing I could do, if in fact, I wanted to get out of this hellhole, and that was to risk my safety by leaving the confinement of the hotel and get to a government office in order to obtain an exit visa.

So with the same two security guards that had escorted my fiancée to the airport, I climbed into an unmarked vehicle with a cloth over my head and I laid in the backseat so as not to be seen by any of the antigovernment protesters.

I was wondering if I was doing the right thing by going to a government building in the midst of what had been going on but wanted to leave the country so desperately, figured it was worth the risk.

This particular building was a short drive from the hotel and the roads were back to some sort of normality after the events of the night before and so the journey took approximately fifteen minutes from the hotel. As we were driving, I started to wish I had called my kids, just to hear their voices. Was I starting to panic? It was a possibility as we had heard from the British Embassy earlier that a couple of British tourists had taken a ride in one of the most questionable taxi companies and had been forced at knife point to hand everything they owned as the taxi driver drove so that the passengers' side was blocked by a brick wall that he had driven up to, thus impeding their potential exiting from the cab in question.

But I am going to be all right, I thought to myself. *I have the security with me. But then what if the security guards could not be trusted?*

No sooner had we embarked on our journey, we been stopped by the police. "So what now?" Fortunately for me, I spoke almost fluent Bahasa Indonesia and could hear the security guard explain that I was an ex-patriot, trying to get to the building that would allow me to obtain an exit visa. My heart was in my mouth right now as I was told to hand over my passport and show my face for positive ID. What if they had decided to confiscate it then where would I be? So many "what ifs?"

I removed my scarf that was covering my head, the police officer looked in at me, looked at my passport, and waived us through.

All I could think of right now was "would I ever get to our sister hotel in Singapore?"

We had arrived at the government building that was surrounded by police and armed guards. It was also full of ex-patriots with the same idea as I had.

How the hell was I going to get out of this shithole of a country with line ups as long as these? Then the security guard pulled me into a room that was off to one side, just inside the building entrance and said to me, "Pak Tony, did you bring some money today?" To which I replied "Yes" and produced U.S. $500. In Indonesia, it was considered a smart thing to have "bribe" money always handy. Today, I had taken the $500 from my in-room safety deposit box for the trip to the airport. He took all $500 and told me to sit down and wait. After approximately fifteen minutes, an official came by to collect my passport. He disappeared and returned ten minutes later with my passport with an exit visa no less.

He seemed happy with the bribe money he had received although I wasn't sure if he had actually been paid the full $500 or not (probably not), but then at this point, I didn't particularly care as the security guard deserved payment for having his contact take such very good care of me. I had my exit visa and so what else could I have purchased that would have been such great value for money? Nothing!

I had resigned myself to the fact that this was a small price to pay for potential freedom. Back at the hotel, I grabbed my overnight bag from the GM's apartment, went to my room, and stuffed a few more bits and pieces into it (along with an additional $500) and went down to my office and met the GM. He looked at my bag and said to me, "Do you have enough stuff in there for a month?" I looked at him somewhat confused. "A month?" I said. "Yes," he replied. "I have just got off the phone to Michel Noblet—our Regional Director of Operations—and he has told me that you are needed in Tahiti at our sister property there to assist in the opening that is scheduled for three months time. I have been in touch with the GM in Singapore, who has booked you on a Qantas flight to Papeete and you leave tomorrow."

I could feel the joy rising within my stomach as well as the stretching of my face as I was obviously smiling from ear to ear "Here is your ticket to Singapore." I looked at him and said, "Thanks."

He shook my hand as hard as I can remember anybody shaking it in the past and he said to me, "Tony, it is I who should thank you because I could not have wished for a stronger man to have stood beside me in the lobby last night as the shit was about to fly. Come on let's go for that beer before you depart for the airport."

I will never forget the feeling of tremendous appreciation one gets when one is given the best compliment from the man I admired the most for his leadership whilst undergoing what was, on reflection, a moment that I could have certainly done without that night before to one that I can sit and relate to today with so much pride in my heart. It really was a remarkable feeling of self-worth and on top of it all I was on my way to Tahiti . . . so how bloody bad was that?

Netraj and I bundled ourselves into the unmarked hotel car, along with my two security buddies, complete with the addition of a machine gun by his side (I mean, where did they get all this shit from?) and we were off.

I can remember looking out of the back window and seeing Jean-Louis waving at us. God, I so wished he was coming with us.

My mate Netraj had brought with him a small radio that he had plugged into his ears. We were about ten minutes away from the hotel when he shrieked a huge, "*Yes!*" and punched the air over and over again.

Apparently, Soeharto had decided to step down from his role as President of Indonesia. "So what do we do now, Pak Tony?" came the question from the security guard. I said, "Keep going, my friend, keep going."

On arriving at the international airport, I could hardly believe my eyes. It was as if the entire armed forces were out on display. There were tanks and armored vehicles around the perimeter, as well as heavily armed troops in full combat gear. The car pulled up and we thanked our security guards for the safe passage to the airport and made our way into the terminal. It was absolute mayhem!

We couldn't find any trolleys to place our bags on and what would have been the point? The entire terminal was jam-packed with all nationalities, all trying to get their bags checked in. In fact, it was impossible to get close to the check-in counter, period. There must have been at least two thousand people, pushing and shoving. There were people carrying suitcases on their heads, trying to inch their way into the front of the lineup. The air conditioning was no longer operational and it was thirty-four degrees Celsius outside; fistfights were breaking out left and right, kids were defecating wherever it took their fancy as getting to a washroom was proving fruitless, the noise was deafening and the stench of poop and urine made me retch. "God only knows how we are going to get out of here!" I shouted at Netraj. It was going to take a miracle.

Hadn't we been through enough already and now this? It seemed hopeless.

We walked until we found a small spot then sat down on our bags.

A little kid came over to within about three feet of us and started to pee up against the wall. I felt like shouting at him but what good would it have done? With so many people around and with just a handful of washrooms available, who could blame him.

We sat there and I wanted to cry again. I asked Netraj if he had brought any money with him (we spoke in French as there were far too many people around us who, quite easily could have understood us in either English or Bahasa Indonesia and who, at the same time, could have quite easily attacked and robbed us of our U.S. currency). It appeared that we had a total of $1,000 between us, and so as the final call was announced for our flight to Singapore, I decided to look for "assistance." It was after approximately two hours later that we were able to access the fiscal counter. As residents of Indonesia, each time you left the country, you had to pay Rp 1,000,000.

I had calculated once that, since having lived in Indonesia for a total of four years (this was my second tour, the first had been five years earlier with my kids), the hotels I had worked in had very generously forked out a total of Rp 75,000.000. You could buy a new Mercedes for that price!

As we approached the fiscal counter, I had the fiscal fee neatly tucked inside my passport; I handed it over to the sleazy little Indonesian chap, when I heard from behind the glass somewhere deep in the back of the office that was filed with the smoke of the clove-flavored cigarettes. "Hey, Pak Tony, *apa kabar*?" I looked as hard as I could to see who it was and then, as if appearing out of the plume of cigarette smoke, came the guy who had earlier issued me with my exit visa. All of a sudden a ray of hope sprang back into my heart because if anybody could get us on an aircraft to anywhere (I didn't very much care where we were headed, just as long as it was out of Indonesia), he was likely to be our best chance.

I said to him in Bahasa, "We need to get through to customs, but we need to check in first." He signaled for us to go into the office. As we pushed our way through the throngs of people so as to get to the office door, I felt Netraj put his $500 into my pocket. He knew as well as I did that things were looking up.

Once inside the office, *my* man, as we were now affectionately referring to him, was all ears as I explained that we had missed the 5:45 p.m. flight to Singapore (I knew that at this point, if there was any chance of us bribing our way onto an aircraft, we most certainly stood a much better chance by being on the other side of customs, as opposed to this side). He explained to me that Singapore Airlines had scheduled two additional jumbo jets and the next flight was supposed to leave at 10:15 p.m. but was full; the flight after this, however, was scheduled to leave at 11:50 p.m. and as far as he could tell, had some spare seats still. I said, "How much would it cost for you to guarantee us two seats on this flight?" He said he would have to pay a lot of people along the way so it would cost me double what I had paid in getting my exit visa. "You mean, you want me to pay you $1,000 to get onto an epoxy airplane to Singapore?" He smiled at me and said, "No, Pak Tony, only double, that's $400, no?"

"You mean you only got paid $200 today?" Then the penny had finally dropped. That asshole of a security guard had pocketed $300 of the $500 I had given toward the cost of obtaining my exit visa.

I took the $500 Netraj had put in my pocket and said, "This is all I have." He smiled, took the money and both our passports and was gone. Again, the "what if's" started to cross my mind but we were so close to getting on an outbound flight that I said to myself, "And what if not?"

It seemed as if an hour had passed before *my* man had returned with our passports and boarding passes, by which time the smoke of the clove-flavored cigarettes had been firmly impregnated our clothes and hair.

"There you are, Pak Tony, you are both confirmed on the 11:50 p.m. flight to Singapore, please follow me, Pak." With this, we left the office and followed him like sheep to the customs officer, who opened my passport, removed the U.S. $100 bill that *my* man had obviously placed in there, stamped both mine and Netraj's passports, and we were on our way. I turned to thank *my* man, but he had left us and he was either on his way home or was relieving some other expat of their U.S. currency, by arranging a safe passage for them also.

We boarded flight SA 94 at 10:45 p.m. The aircraft must have only recently been commissioned into service as the leather seats smelled as if they had only just been installed. We were sat on the upper deck of this 747, I was sitting by the window. The pretty air hostess came by and asked us what we wanted to drink. I ordered a triple gin and tonic. Normally, when flying Singapore airlines, they would not have entertained a "triple" of anything, but I would have imagined that this air hostess had been briefed on the potentially difficult day we had all experienced and so accommodated my request.

At exactly 11:50 p.m., our magnificent beast of an aircraft was pushed back and within fifteen minutes, we were screaming down the runway. As the wheels left the ground, I could feel a stream of tears running down my face, because yes, I was actually going to see my kids and fiancée again!

As if sensing my joy and relief, Netraj said something to me that still resonates in my mind today. It was almost the same thing I had asked him less than twenty-four hours earlier, while we stood together in the hotel lobby. "Are you okay, because I am?" I couldn't answer him as I was so choked up! I just stared out of the window and watched as the ground disappeared from beneath us.

All he said to me was, "Touché, my friend . . . touché."

CHAPTER TWO

Where It Had All Begun Twenty-Seven Years Earlier

I WAS LAYING ON MY bed in Arncliffe, which is the name of a road on a housing estate by the name of Wildridings, in a town called Bracknell, Berkshire, in England (our house at the time) musing over the fact that the night before I had willingly given up my virginity to a girl by the name of Sue, and on inspection of the "down bellows" was disappointed to find that nothing had changed. God only knows what I was expecting to find! Anything that would have indicated that a momentous challenge had been noted and that my life would never be the same as a result.

Well, the fact that I am writing about it now is testament that it did. The song at the time was "I'm Not in Love" by 10cc (circa 1972) only goes to prove that she did leave a deep impression. I had lent her my 10cc album hoping that one day, we would be able to sit in our lounge together, admiring our wonderful children, reminiscing the old days while listening to our album.

I was like a kid that had fallen in love with ice cream for the first time in his life and was addicted to it as a result. My wife Ni can attest to this and I am lucky to be able to report that Ni also loves ice cream.

"You know sex was only so that you have babies." (Brother did I ever make one wrong turn on that one when I was in the church for the first time.) In fact, I was so scared to have let down the congregation or I should have walked out as soon as I heard the music.

Anyway, whilst on my bed and contemplating my next move on Sue, I was unaware that the necklace I had given her two months earlier, as a sign of my undying love for her, was placed on the entrance desk to her house along with the record I had bought for her (I thought she loved the song but I had failed to study the lyrics), ready to be handed back to me as a sign of her disappointment of my performance the previous night. I took it on the chin as any respectable man would followed by my nonchalant comment which was the icing on the cake. "Well you were the worst lay I have ever had and there have been a shit load let me tell you." I didn't have the heart to say she was my first encounter I had ever had and was totally unqualified to make such a statement, but boy did it feel good at the time. I came home to Arncliffe a tad despondent trying to determine if my heart was completely broken or just my pride bruised beyond repair.

As the hormones were trying to sort themselves out, or me, and not sure what was going on, Dad came into the bedroom with the profoundest of questions. "Son, what do you think you would like to do career wise?" I thought this was a bit inconsiderate and out of the blue because hey, I was only seventeen years of age and felt that this was far too complicated a question, let alone a decision to be considered at such a tender age. I had lost my cherry the night before, to whom I thought was the most beautiful woman in the world and my Dad was being so insensitive as to ask what I was preparing to do with the rest of my life.

I proceeded to tell Dad that I really wanted to be was a pilot in the RAF but because I was partially blind in one eye, had been informed that my chances as a result were next to none. I had no real idea as to what channel my life was not headed nor which career path I was to pursue.

My interests at this point were finding ways to earn enough money to run my Morris Minor that would burn fifteen miles to the gallon along with two pints of oil.

I had purchased it for the princely sum of five quid and I can remember Dad showing it to me in his workshop yard in Crowthorne. It was a 1955 model that had a split windscreen for a front window and the little orange indicators that would pop out of the side of the vehicle as you indicated as to which way you would be turning. It was bottle green and had just been fitted with a reconditioned engine, a bit musty smelling inside due to a leak that was never officially determined as to its origin.

Within a short while, the paint had been taken back to its almost previous glory with what we called back then "T cut" (T cut would assist in removing the dead paint from the surface to assist in bringing back the paint to a beautiful shine). The interior was made of green leather and once polished, masked the damp smell that had started to diminish with the aid of a hair dryer and a rather long extension cord from our house to the parking lane.

The engine would strain tremendously at forty-five miles per hour and a light plume of blue smoke would appear from the exhaust pipe. Needless to say, forty-five miles an hour was it! This car was my pride and joy and can recall being somewhat fortunate at being one of the only sixth formers, who had just recently left school to actually own one.

On leaving for Switzerland, it was sad to have to part with it but did so at a price of seventy-five quid!

So to cut a long story short, Dad has asked if I had ever thought about becoming a chef! *What, a poof in white gear with a stupid hat and a lithsp! Not for me, big boy*, I thought to myself. On reflection, wondered if my wizardry with the sponge cakes under Mum's supervision had had an influence on Dad's thoughts and had also played an important part in his question.

Dad's bookkeeper had a son who had started out in the culinary world and had done well, and had even progressed into a higher management position and maybe he was a chap that we should speak to.

I really hadn't thought about it but was pleased when Dad had suggested I meet a qualified chef for a chat.

The following Monday, Mum and Dad had kitted me out in my chef's white gear and I was off to the Reading College of Technology to start my career as a chef.

I think the chef's attire may have almost cleaned out their bank account as Dad had very kindly warned me that I had joked around at school for far too long and this was the best chance I had at a career in life.

College was fun and challenging at the same time. We had some of the best lecturers and some of the worst. It was an eye-opener for me but Mum and Dad had put their faith in me, so it was the best I could do to give it my best shot.

While in college, it was recommended that we get weekend jobs, the purpose of which was twofold—beer and date money (naturally), as well as valuable on the job experience. It was true that there were far too many potential chefs that were well qualified on paper after having left college but, in every regard, were totally unprepared for what the big hospitality world had to offer. As time went on, I began to realize just how unfriendly and unforgiving the hospitality world was going to be. Many of us "qualified chefs" would fall by the wayside within the first year as really the kitchen was too hot to bear, in more ways than one.

I studied with keenness and worked hard at my weekend job at a little restaurant in Benfield called "The Wooden Hut." This was a quaint little restaurant of approximately fifty seats and had a limited menu. Here I learned how to royally cremate ten ducks for the evening's service, cook whitebait so that as opposed to them being individually fried, turned into a solid mass of tiny fish, and boiled the living daylights out of new potatoes so that they were salty beyond the Red Sea. Here, I also learned that in one of the owner's eyes (who incidentally played for the other team), I was a "f——ing" waste of space, an idiot and would never make it in the culinary world. Ha . . . did I have a plan for him—I stayed away from ducks, whitebait, and new potatoes for the duration of my tenure there and did very well as a result.

I also got to work at the Masonic Lodge where I gained valuable experience in the catering of large numbers (up to one hundred and seventy five if I am not mistaken). The reason I have added this is because the other morning I woke up with a smile on my face as I recalled and what I think was a true reflection of the colorful people who adorn the hospitality industry.

Anyway, I was a part-timer there, working Saturdays only, alongside the executive chef by the name of Mike, as well as an apprentice by the name of Dave. Well, this particular Saturday it was Dave's birthday and after service was complete, they (bartenders as well as all the servers) grabbed poor Dave and dunked him in the Bain-Marie (this is a large bath of water used for keeping pots of soups and sauces warm during service). There was a rather mature (almost naturally blond) large-breasted waitress by the name of Trudy, who had decided that his chef checkered pants as well as his underwear should be ripped from his body. I stood a good twelve feet away as Dave was hanging on to his underwear, as if his very life depended on it. All I could see was a lot of splashing water, and as if in slow motion, Dave's pants went up high above his head. Then Trudy stood back, looking down at his manhood with her hands over her face in disbelief, only for a second, then shrieked at the top of her voice, "Jesus Christ, look at the size of that bloody thing—it's no wonder he looks so thin and pale, it must be feeding off him."

I only lasted another week and resigned amid the fear that this would happen to me at any time and, in any event, how was I going to compete with Dave's magnificent trophy of manhood?

The truth of the matter was that I could not, even if I had wanted to; so rather than suffer the indignation of Trudy's comments, I had decided to call it quits.

After two years of college incidences that included one of the students, by the name of Trevor who, by the way most definitely batted for the other team, was looking at me across the stoves and asking me if he could squeeze my eggs and then blowing me a kiss—I beat the crap out of him at the bus stop after college that day—to one of the lecturers being held up for sexual assault at having grabbed Deb's boobs in front of us all . . . what was he thinking?

So having been awarded male student of the year, it was time to move on.

Where would this incredible journey lead me? I had been told by so many people that in the hospitality trade, the world really was your oyster, so I decided just how much I liked oysters and proceeded to the principal's office for some advice.

I had so much respect for Mrs. Fellows. She somehow managed to keep that quality of "grace" about her whilst having to work with the perverts and drunkards (often referred to as our lecturers) of our college.

Mrs. Fellows had always given me glowing year-end reports and so I thought a trip to her office could possibly provide me with an edge over the other ruffians in my class as to the career opportunities the hospitality had to offer. The gamble paid off and we sat down for a chat. "Have you ever thought of Switzerland?" she said to me.

CHAPTER THREE

Switzerland Here We Come

S O I WAS OFF TO rub shoulders with some of the best culinary masters in the world (they had the reputation for this). Mum and Dad were delighted that I was off to a stupendous start to my culinary career. All I could think of was, how many of the barmaids (who had the reputation of being buxom ladies) would I have under my belt before the year was out?

I had left the UK with the absolute wrong impression of both the barmaids as well as these Swiss culinary masters. It was July 11, 1973 and the sun was blaring down at me as I was dropped off at Heathrow for a very sad farewell by Mum and Dad. Well I know it was a sad day for my Mum and I but could never figure out if it was as sad for Dad. (Note to self, next time you see Dad, ask him why he had a grin from ear to ear as I went through to the departure lounge.)

Typically, as is the case in most colleges, they will try to find you employment as you conclude your course so that you are not thrust out to line up with the ranks and file of the unemployed

I laid in my bed the night before, looking up at the ceiling thinking to myself. "I have lived here all my life, never been away from my parents or sisters, have always had beautifully cooked English food, lived five minutes up the road from a great pub, had great neighbors, aunts, and uncles left and right, had my little old car that Dad had managed to get for a fiver. I don't think I want to leave and go to Zürich to work at the Bahnhof Buffet." (I spoke French, in Zürich they converse in German).

How would I be able to express myself, let alone understand what these great chefs were going to teach me? Shit, how am I going to get out of this mess. Suddenly I felt quite lonely and most venerable. I had been spoiled rotten, so far, that's for sure.

I thought about this all through the night and before finally dropping off to sleep, resigned myself to the fact that I was at the point of no return. I owed it to Mum and Dad to get out there and get on with it!

After getting off the plane and going through customs at Zürich International Airport, I noticed how everything smelt so strange and looked so different. I went to catch a tram into the city center and looked up at the clouds, even they looked different from the ones we had in England. I felt a pang of insecurity but it had to be done.

As I climbed up into the tram I had to pay four Francs (coins) into the machine. I only had five ten Franc notes. What the hell was I going to do now? The driver of the tram took my ten Franc note, gave me four in exchange and kept the rest. "Bastard. You wait till my mum hears about this." Git!

"Sheet down you little English Schrimp und have zee correct monies next time yah!"

I was just so glad God had taken to him with the ugly bat more than once and that the Francs he had swindled me out of would go to some great cause like buying him some toothpaste.

"I want to go home," I whispered to myself. And a lovely old lady sitting beside me said and a deep gruff voice, "But you have only just got here, my dear," and proceeded to put her hand on my leg.

I sat perfectly still for an additional fifteen minutes staring at her hand. This Switzerland idea was getting worse by the minute. Am I to be accosted by a seventy-five-year-old mountain goat while I was still only seventeen? What was wrong with the world; this country is full of smelly, ugly old perverts. And here I thought I had left all of those back in England at my college in the form of the lecturers.

Bahnhof the swindler announced. Thank God! I slipped out from under the old woman's hand, not without a last squeeze. "See you later, yah?"

Not if I have my bloody way you won't! I thought to myself.

Now what do I do? It was pitch-black; nobody spoke any English and I have to live with this for a year. I put my suitcase down and stared at this huge monument they called the Bahnhof.

This is the German name for Station.

So this was the Bahnhof. I sat on my suitcase in despair. What on earth was I thinking when I agreed to come to this place. It smelled different from England, the roads and curb were painted differently.

There were plenty of bars with tables and chairs outside with that horrible stench of those French Gauloises cigarettes. Oh, how I wish I could just walk into my local pub in good old Wildridings back in the UK and be able to smell the scent of Piccadilly blues (a cigarette brand) and order a pint of Courage bitter.

I walked along the Bahnhof Strasse with perspiration flowing down the small of my back. It was hot and I was tired and wanted to check into a hotel for a safe night's sleep. I was supposed to report for work at 9: 00a.m. the next day and didn't have a clue what to do next. This Bahnhof was certainly overbearing and as I walked closer to it, the smell of the food being prepared excited my appetite and I had forgotten how hungry I actually felt. I need food and beer, but one thing at a time. How was I going to find my accommodation? This was by far, one of the loneliest nights I would ever experience, I later found out.

Wandering back and forth in front of this colossal building, I had started to contemplate a trip back to the airport, a possible restless night in one of Zürich airport's finest lounge chairs that adorned the departure lounge, and then a quick flight home to England. But then I thought better of it as I remembered Dad's impression of a Cheshire cat as we had said our farewells.

The taxis in Zürich looked very much like they had all been produced by the local Mercedes Benz sweatshop. Every one of them seemed full of passengers and the thought of getting ripped off once again, by one of Zürich's most elite cab drivers had me rethinking. Besides, everybody in the UK had congratulated me on this unique opportunity of having the chance to work with the world's greatest chefs. I was definitely giving in to early. I owed to everyone to stay put. Our neighbor in Arncliffe, Carol George, a wonderful lady, had given me a wooden spoon as a parting gift to "Stir your thoughts of home with." I couldn't possible go back now, even Carol thought I could manage it so; the straw had broken the camel's back, I was going to stay whatever the outcome.

I had, while looking for a taxi, inadvertently walked passed what turned out to be the staff entrance to the Bahnhof. I stopped and looked at the men leaving. They were happy and joking. What a comfortable feeling that must have been to have completed a day's work, knowing full well you had a job to return to the following day. I envied them so much. I was practically soiling my pants thinking about my first night's sleep and then realized I had so much to do and learn. Was this really the opportunity of a life time I had been presented? I wasn't to know until I have at least given it a chance.

My desire for a beer and something to eat grew ever stronger in my stomach and the constant raucous of everybody in the bar was starting to get at me. Work couldn't have been that great surely. The thought of a beer and a bratwurst was getting the better of me and I decided that if I was going to sleep, it would be easier on a full stomach. With this I proceeded to walk into the Bahnhof station buffet. I wondered if I had enough money on me to be able to afford some sustenance when I heard a gruff German voice speaking in English to a fellow of his shouting, "Yah unt the English fellow didn't make it here, ha!"

"Bloody steak and kidney pie was probably too scared and stayed at home wid his muma, yah." As they all seemed to be splitting a gut over what appeared to be the lack of the presence among the troops of some poor English sod, I wondered how many other poor English bastards had been led to this humiliating slaughter.

The penny dropped so hard I could feel it rattling around in my underpants along with my balls. Shit, it was me they were laughing at! Who else could have been so stupid to have boarded a bus with only paper currency in his pocket and no loose change *and* allow some decrepit old mountain goat to have her hand on his knee for almost fifteen minutes?

My hunger pains soon diminished as I felt the obvious pains of humiliation run throughout my body. Where were the bloody taxis when you needed them?

If ever there was a time to put one's hand up and finally be counted, it was now.

But what would they be calling me next, "A piece of Roast beef with a soggy Yorkshire pudding?"

There in itself the decision to stay in this strange country, was carved in stone for this young lad from England and now I had answered my own question.

The English were renowned for culinary delicacies such as steak and kidney pies along with roast beef and Yorkshire puddings (which I had to admit was one of my favorite meals) and wait for it, *fish and chips*, not to mention toad in the hole and Irish stew. Oh my god. I could hear it now, within no time I would inherit the title of "chip butty" whilst grafting among these masters of the culinary universe.

My knees began to wobble as I smiled at these chaps (I had assumed they were from the kitchen), raised my hand and chirped out, "I think I may be the steak and kidney pie you are looking for."

I have never, to this day, had the privilege of seeing seven burly foreigners almost cry instantaneously and have tears flow from their eyes so involuntarily. Two of the chaps, who I later found out were from Barcelona, were choking as they roared with laughter. Frenchie, who later became a longtime pal of mine, actually turned around to the edge of the bridge and, as a result of his laughter, threw up what must have been everything he had consumed that day. (The deluge made a familiar slapping sound as it hit the river surface below.) He had obviously found it very amusing too.

What a bunch of assholes! I thought to myself.

They had all had a good day at work and apparently, I had just made it one of the best they were likely to have in a very long time.

"Are you zee guy from England working here?"

I puckered up the old British courage to make it look as if I was totally in control, knew exactly what this was all about, and had just sat down for a breather.

"Yes, this is me."

"You look lost and worried!"

"I just need to know where to go from here."

"Come and follow me," said one German fellow. The rest seemed to go their separate ways. If only I were a bit bigger and had bigger balls, I could quite happily swung at one of them but that idea was soon not to be reckoned with when I remembered there were more of them than I. In any case, I was a peaceful, non-confrontational chef who just wanted to get to bed—alone. All I wanted was a beer and something to eat, was this too much to ask for?

The wrinkled mountain goat, once again, seemed to appear before me.

I had to carry my own suitcase which weighed a ton and seemed to be at least three times my size.

As it turned out, Wolfe was a very pleasant German guy who decided that on route to our accommodation, we should stop and have a beer. It was, to this day, one of the most memorable beverages I had ever had the pleasure to have consumed. The bar was on the side of the Bahnhof Strasse. It was full of foreigners and so getting used to the rambling of German and Swiss dialects was something I realized I would soon have to get used to. And the sooner the better if I was going to stand any chance of survival. The stench of the Gauloises prevailed until I could smell it in my hair an on my clothes, which were now wet with perspiration. The suitcase had been heavier than I had imagined and the walk to the bar one I could have done without. As I drank the beer, my thoughts of the bus driver having ripped me off by having cheated me out of some Francs subsided but the thought of the old lady, who had almost guaranteed we would meet again, was forefront in my mind

I scanned the bar checking every face for the wrinkled experience. She was not to be found, but in any event, I accepted a second beer from my new friend Wolfe, just in case.

Wolfe, I had later found out, had worked in many of the great hotels in Germany. At two hundred and eighty pounds (if he was an ounce) and only twenty-four years of age, he was what I had imagined a gentle giant would be. His beard was thin and blond, as was his curly hair (that was longer than I would have given the Swiss credit for allowing, in these great kitchens of the world). His English was impeccable and something I had come to appreciate. I knew after our third beer, he was going to be my friend. He spoke of his girlfriend, Beatrice, affectionately and often. I was relieved my new friend was not a "noofter" as I had felt nothing but unease since arriving in Zürich and I felt as if I deserved to feel at home. After my sixth beer, I felt as if Wolfe was the brother I had always wanted and I had then decided we should probably head off to our accommodation. I couldn't wait to get my head into a plush, clean, fragrant-smelling pillow.

On arriving at our dormitory, we climbed into what seemed to be one of the strangest elevators I had ever experienced. You pressed the button, the door opened as if you were walking into a very tiny washroom, then the door closed behind you and on selecting the desired floor (ours was the third) the whole thing moved, but with nothing between us and the wall; so in short, you could touch the wall as you went from floor to floor. *Strange,* I thought to myself. But then this is a foreign country so what was one to expect. Little did I know that these were all over the UK and I had just not experienced them before.

Upon arriving at the third floor, I was shown to my room that I was to share with three other chaps—Frenchie, whose psychedelic "yodel" over the bridge back at the bar was impressive, to say the least, the big Español, and Wolfe. Thank God Wolfe was going to be there to protect me from these barbarians.

Frenchie was absolutely shit faced and Español wasn't far behind him, but they made me feel very welcome by offering me a beer. It was close to 10:00 p.m. and I so desperately wanted to go to sleep but felt that if I was going to be accepted within this unruly bunch of hoodlums, then the least I could do was play along, and in any event, how much sleep was I going to get while these guys were still in the partying mood?

The dorm was so warm that Frenchie was sitting on the edge of the window which as it turned out was the ideal spot because as I related my tram ride from the airport to the Bahnhof and my terrifying experience with the "mountain goat," he erupted into an uncontrollable fit of laughter, hurling and additional psychedelic yawn out of the window and onto the street below. Español, I swear, must have a pissed himself and my brother Wolfe laughed so hard, he had tears running down his face.

Wolfe looked at me and said, "You are going to get on with us just fine, my friend."

This was music to my ears and as I lay on top of my bed, in just a T-shirt and undershorts (it was far too hot to wear anything else), I thought to myself that I might like it here after all. I had made three friends so far, so how bad was that?

My bed was comfortable and my pillow was divine and it smelt so fresh. I closed my eyes and slept like a baby.

CHAPTER FOUR

My First Day in the "Real World"

WOLFE'S ALARM WENT OFF AT 5:30 a.m. and we were both showered and on our way to the Bahnhof, which incidentally was only a five minute walk away, by 6:30 a.m. I was a bit concerned that Frenchie and Español hadn't made it to the bathroom only to be reassured by Wolfe that they both had the day off on this particular day.

Wolfe took me to the personnel office and introduced me to the assistant personnel manager, who could quite possibly have been the daughter of mountain goat but this time I smiled at the thought of Frenchie's reaction to my rendition of events, so I felt at peace with the world.

She started waffling on at me in German, and I said very politely, "Excuse me, but I don't speak German." Well, if looks could have killed?

"What? Not a vord?"

To which I foolishly replied, "Nien."

"Well vot are you doing here zen?"

I felt so tempted to stand up tall and proud ready to announce in my finest Basel Fawlty accent with my right arm at a forty-five degree angle, with my left index finger firmly positioned over my upper lip, screaming, "I am from Germany und am a Spy zat is on a mission to determine actually how many of ze mountain goats you haf living here in ze city yah." But what I actually said was, "I am here to work in the kitchen." To which she replied, "Well good luck as ze chef hates English people."

"Well," I said to myself, "that was a nice personal touch and one that makes me feel a whole lot better." I should make it part of my mission whilst here in Switzerland to ensure this woman is blindfolded, marched into a courtyard and on a cold and miserable morning and —shot. This way, all the other poor bastards who should have suffered her wrath can in fact be spared.

It was only after approximately three days of my introduction to this "whale" of a women that I was able to determine that she was very unaffectionately referred to as the "Bismarck," not for her killing ability, but more from the fact that her facial features (nose and ears and cheek bones) were somehow formed in such a way that she looked as if she was built for speed, that was in fact until you looked at her from behind, when her arse definitely looked as if she was the width of the Bismarck.

I thought to myself, *Where the bloody hell would you start with one as big as this?*

Realizing it was not a problem I had to concern myself with, I ended up following her (Mrs. B) to the staff cafeteria for lunch where I was treated to a pork schnitzel along with some french fries and a glass of carbonated apple juice. The schnitzel was nothing more than a cut of neck that was probably fifty percent fat thirty percent lean meat and the balance was breadcrumbs. I picked at it and when I had finished with it the cafeteria lady said to me, "Vot is wrong, you don't like the schnitzel zat ze chef haf prepared for you. He is not going to be very happy sat you have not eat it all, it is his best seller out zer in zee Bahnhof." At this point in the juncture, I had promptly detected what, I thought, could possibly have been a conspiracy against me because I was a limey within the world of the most elite culinarians. I mean, could this "culinary wizard" be giving the cafeteria server

Helga, a bit of his own pork schnitzel (who was to know or care?). I almost didn't choke back the words that came straight to my mind, those being, "You mean, we actually serve that shit to the customers?"

I was in enough trouble already, having picked at the chef's specialty that *he* had cooked for me, to pieces, and all I had done was dissect it, as if it had been a frog in a biology class. I started to feel sick and suddenly wished I was sitting at the dinner table in Arncliffe with a nice beef casserole in front of me. I was definitely feeling very sick, not because of the food but more as a result at the thought of meeting the chef within the hour. I went to the washroom. Needless to say that being in a strange country with "it" coming out of both ends in what only can be described as relentless abandon was for me, almost the stepping stone between losing it and grooving with it.

After lunch, I was escorted to the uniform room to be fitted with my "whites." There was this beautifully blond woman by the name of Gertrude I believe, with whom I immediately fell in love with. She has such an innocent smile and such a pretty face. I was heartbroken when I found out that Frenchie was bonking her. What a waste!

In any event, had I known my tenure at the Bahnhof was going to be as short as it was, I felt that it was probably for the better.

I was taken to the kitchen and can only describe my absolute amazement as to the amount of controlled chaos that seemed to prevail. There were pots and pans flying all over the place, with shrieks of screaming coming from the monster on the pass (this had to be the chef) as he was coordinating the lunch service. I saw one of the apprentices, who was manning the grill section, place a royally buggered pork chop on a plate, only to be given a right backhander from the chef, along the side of his left ear that sent his hat flying. This was accompanied by a load of abuse that could only have be translated into what was obviously a warning that if it were to ever happen again, he would be hanging from his nuts somewhere for all to see. This resulted in an uproar of laughter until the chef looked back at his brigade with a threatening glance that brought the laughter to a hasty end.

Naturally, I hadn't stopped laughing until it was too late and the glare that was accorded to me sent a chill down my spine.

I needed the washroom again, but this time it had to be quick!

On my return, the panic had seemed to have subsided, and there I stood all alone, in this massive area of white tiles, steam, waiting for something to happen—what, I was not sure, but I was not going to introduce myself the monster. Then out from the garde-manger (cold food preparation area), appeared my new buddy Wolfe, who quickly whisked me into his area where I remained for the rest of the day. Little had I known that Wolfe was the chef de partie (head of this particular section) of the garde-manger section and word had got around the kitchen that I had not liked my lunch and so he assumed it was in my best interest to be kept out of the sight of the chef, at least until the next day.

So I was set the task of chopping up some onions for a potato salad, then slice some tomatoes for a tomato and cheese salad and make the lemon tea. This was the beverage all the cooks used to drink and was kept in an old milk urn that was positioned inside the main cooler that must have been half the size of a football pitch and was the largest of three.

I remember being given the recipe to follow and it meant boiling up a pot full of water. But this meant I would have leave the cool confines of the cold kitchen (the garde-manger) and reach into the fray of the hot kitchen where *he* was going to be, but as luck would have it, *he* had gone for the rest of the afternoon and wouldn't be back until 5:30 p.m. which is when our day finished.

My tea-making skills were tested and proven and the beverage was considered a resounding success. I was continuously checking my watch hoping that 5:30 p.m. would not be too far away when Wolfe shouted at me, "Quick get inside the refrigerator, Schnel, Schnel." It was the old bastard who had returned early from his break and he was looking for me! What should I do? Stay in the cooler among all the meat that was hanging there, waiting to be butchered, or take my fate into my hands and boldly go out and confront the old bastard. As I stood there contemplating what move would be best, the door to the cooler swung open. I needed the washroom again but where would I go; I managed a little fart and that seemed to relax me for a while. Took a big gulp of air and as the figure in white appeared at the door I started to shake only to realize it was Español. He had been called in as the night crew were short a member and so was getting double time for working the shift.

We both logged out at 5;30 p.m. and I decided to take my new "brother" to the bar for a drink and where upon I think I fell in love yet again with what appeared to be the most beautiful female I had ever yet to meet. She was tall, blond, and beautiful with a full body. She walked toward the table and with the quickness of the eye bent down and kissed Wolfe on the cheek.

"My darling, I would like for you to meet my new friend and culinary colleague—all the way from England—Tony."

It was his girlfriend, Beatrice.

But how, I thought to myself, *did this blond lump of lard, who weighed an absolute ton, find a beauty like Beatrice. I mean, what did he have that I couldn't possibly have?*

Then the voice of Trudy from the Masonic lodge started reverberating through my head, almost like an old witch's cackle that kept saying to me, "Jesus Christ, look at the size of that bloody thing, it's no wonder he looks so thin and pale, it must be feeding off him."

Maybe I should rethink my plan as it had pertained to all these women I had planned to seduce whilst here in Switzerland.

I slept pretty well that night despite having woken up three times to measure my pecker's length using Wolfe's ruler that lay beside his desk that he used for his technical drawing gear, I mean, what did he need it for? The bastard was probably hung like a bloody moose, and how could he do it with a belly as large as his? And where was the bloody justice in the world?

Well, it wasn't lying beside *me* that was for sure!

CHAPTER FIVE

"D" Day

MY TRAVELING ALARM CLOCK WOKE me at 5:30 a.m. and as I moved around in my bed, I felt a sickening pain in my stomach, as if I knew something bad was going to happen. I felt sick with the thought of finally meeting up with the executive chef. I couldn't avoid him forever, and I felt as if today would be the day. As I turned toward the window, I saw Wolfe. He was butt naked, on all fours, with his head halfway under his bed, looking for the second of a pair of socks whilst showing off his crown jewels and not in the least bit concerned that what he had for a manhood; turned out to be a little less than what amounted to be three button mushrooms—two for his testicles and the other for his . . . well you can imagine the rest. I thought to myself with a smile. Hung like a moose indeed, more like a bleeding *mouse*. And I looked under the covers to check mine and concluded that at a conservative estimate, I had at least four times what he was packing, but then, how had he managed to corner such a beauty in Beatrice? Definitely something to ponder about but then, the sickening feeling in my stomach had returned as I thought about the day that was going to ensue.

Wolfe had found his sock, thank goodness, as the sight of lard ass was starting to make me feel even sicker than I was already feeling, and so with this dragged myself out of bed ad headed to the bathroom. As I looked in the mirror, I thought to myself, *You're looking a bit green around the gills, my man, perhaps you should go back to bed.* Only to be told by my subconscious that I was really kidding myself and the sooner I got it over and done with, the better it would be.

I entered into the kitchen and walked up to the chef's office, peered through the office door window and there he sat, without this hat on sporting a cleanly shaven, shiny bald head. I gulped, held my breath, and knocked on the door. He turned and looked at me; I felt as if my number was up as he got out of his chair. My God, he was much bigger up close and must have been at least two hundred and fifty lbs and at least six feet four inches tall. He opened his mouth and grunted something that I wrongly mistook for a signal to enter his office. I proceeded to walk in and he stood there blocking the door; I bumped into him and realizing my mistake briskly and took a step backward. This man was as solid as a rock and so overbearing in many ways. Then he said in a very thick German accent, "So you think zat when an apprentice screws up a dish, zat it is funny yah?" Shit, I had forgotten that the previous day he had caught me smiling as the young lad who had copped a right hander after presenting him with a royally buggered pork chop. I was starting to tremble a tad and with the force of a sergeant major on a drill court shouted, "No, Chef, not at all, Chef!" And with that he just waved me away, as if I was a puff of smoke.

Ignorant SOB, I thought to myself. And then realized that the dreaded introduction was over and on reflection, should have considered myself quite fortunate to have gotten away without a mark on my body (for now, in any event).

I went to my post and got to the first job at hand, making the tea for the rest of the brigade. Surely this wasn't to be my vocation in life, to be the tea waller? Well, at least I wasn't being trusted with cooking on the grill yet!

"So?" Wolfe said to me as I was making the tea.

"So what?"

"Did he rip your balls off for refusing to eat that pork schnitzel that he cooked for you?"

"No," I replied. "Why?"

"He will, when the time is right. I promise you he will."

Wolfe was starting to turn into an asshole but then this was the kitchen and it really was a matter of "the strong survives," so I had better toughen up if in fact I was going to survive.

Then it happened! The sous chef was screaming at the top of his

Voice, "Bring ze English one here." *One.* I thought to myself. One? As if marching out to greet the firing squad, I gingerly made my way to where the Sous chef was standing and said,

"Yes, Chef."

He pointed to the grill and handed me a set of tongs and said, "The chef vants you to cook his lunch und he is having pork chop!"

I could almost feel my bum cheeks quiver as I was given the pork chop. "Now?"

"No, next week—you stupid limey!"

With this rather rude reaction to what I considered to be a perfectly normal question, I seasoned the pork chop and placed it on the hottest part of the grill; after two minutes, turned it ninety degrees so that it would have the pleasant markings of a nicely grilled chop, left it there for two more minutes, then flipped it over onto the not-so-hot area of the grill and cooked it for seven minutes, then rotated it an additional ninety degrees and cooked it for another seven minutes, then prodded it to make sure it was cooked through and then presented it to the sous chef.

He looked at it, shrugged his shoulders, and placed it on a plate that was full of vegetables and marched it into the chef's office. The wait was unbearably long. The right side of my head started to hurt as if I had just received a right hander, but it turned to be my imagination was playing havoc with me. The chef finished his pork chop, marched out of his office, and left the kitchen with not as much as a "nice" or "good job," not even a "kiss my ass." Then I thought to myself, *What if he has gone to throw up in the bathroom?*

Nobody ever knew why he had left the kitchen, but he came back looking healthy enough and so I breathed a sigh of relief. I never knew whether or not he had enjoyed his pork chop, but then realized that no news was in fact, good news.

The following day, the chef had not come to work as he had contracted a dose of food poisoning. Apparently, his wife had prepared him some sushi for his dinner and it was this that had kept him up all night, screaming down the big white telephone. For a moment, I had imagined that my brief, professional culinary career had come to a grinding halt, but it appeared it had not.

I had been spared the indignation of having potentially poisoned the chef.

The chef was nowhere to be seen on day two and I was reveling in the rumor that it was, in fact, my pork chop that had brought the mighty monster to his knees.

I didn't know that this day would be a milestone within my career, for two reasons basically, and they were as follows. This particular day, I had witnessed some of the worst food I could ever have imagined leave our particular kitchen (of which there were a total of three within the Bahnhof) which included veal face and cheeks, along with pig's ears and testicles, and of course, the chef's famous pork schnitzel, that I had decided that this was not what I had come to Switzerland to learn to cook.

On top of this, I once again, was not in chef's good books.

The reason for this was that each day, between the soup chef's section and the pass (this was where the food would be distributed to the servers), there used to be a little brown mouse that would contemplate—what was referred to by the kitchen brigade as the daily 4:00 p.m. dash. As it did this, they (the kitchen brigade) would wait for it and then scare the shit out of it by hitting their wooden spoons just behind it, as it made its dash to safety.

Well, nobody told me this and as I stood there, determined to rid this culinary nightmare of a critter, that this was considered the chef's little "munchkin." The little shit had decided to make a run for it. I was perfectly positioned just before the pass, and there he was. Beady eyes with what looked like the fear of God in him and he was off. The other cooks were playing the game (of which I had yet to be privy to the rules) by whacking the ground behind him, as he made this desperate dash for freedom.

Well, as it happened, the little brown critter was darting from left to right, and I had successfully anticipated his change of direction; and with a big *smack* of the wooden spoon that I had commandeered from the wash up guy, saw its head depart from its body. I raised my arms in jubilation with a loud *yes!* as if I had just scored the winning goal in a hockey final, only to have the entire brigade look at me as if I had killed their best friend, within the entire world.

Was I now to be ostracized from the entire Bahnhof kitchen as a result of my expert and yet painless execution of this brown critter? Couldn't they see that I had rid the world of a potential reason for a catastrophic food poisoning outbreak? (Something one might have assumed the chef would have considered given his present condition!)

It was now so obvious to me that I could no longer be part of this culinary "enterprise." I mean, all it was, was a mouse (something I thought my friend Wolfe could have related to but to no avail).

The reasoning in my own mind as to why this little creature had met an early demise had been drawn from my training with the drunks and perverts (my culinary lecturers), and it meant absolutely nothing to these people. It appeared I was a murderer and had killed the chef's little "munchkin" and it looked as if I was at the point of being ostracized as a result.

Upon returning to my dorm that day, I had noticed a piece of paper with handwriting in red with the words *MURDERER* placed on the door as I entered. Surely this was not meant for me, I mean it was just a bloody mouse.

That evening the boys returned from work and as I laid in my bed, greeted them with an, "All right?" To which the response was a cold nothing.

"That was it," I had decided. "I had to get out of this place once and for all."

I certainly could not return to the kitchen and face the chef.

No, as sad as it was, my experience among the masters of the culinary world had come to an unprecedented, abrupt end.

I started to pack my suitcase and not a word was said from my friends. Now what was I to do? *Head for the hills.*

CHAPTER SIX

The Hills are Alive, With the Sound of Music?

WHAT A STUPID SONG TITLE, I had thought to myself upon reluctantly watching this movie. More so now than I had ever given credit to a song before.

On seeing me pack, the boys had decided it was time for a chat and so took me to a new bar that had some of those "buxom wenches" I had dreamed of, with boobs bulging from all directions. They explained to me that the chef was absolutely livid with me as I had successfully separated his little munchkin's head from its body in one foul strike but that I had become a sort of a "kitchen" hero for having the balls to have carried out such an execution with such precision, but I explained to them that the only reason I had done such a thing was because nobody had been kind enough to explain the rules to me and that we were supposed to miss the bloody thing, and so in my eyes, I had become this legendary kitchen hero by default. Well, this had Frenchie in fits of laughter, and luckily, it was still the early part of the afternoon and so there was no psychedelic yawn to follow, which I thought was a shame as it would have cheered me up no end.

I then went on to explain them that in my opinion, the Bahnhof Buffet was just a glorified cafeteria for me and this was not what I had come to Switzerland to learn about. But my friend Wolfe pointed out to me, "There was always the Etage, which is where the banquet food is prepared and this is most certainly the place you needed to be as this was where some of the finest cuisine would be prepared."

Which was true, but I had heard that every cook in the kitchen wanted to go to the Etage and this Bahnhof Buffet was just a stepping stone but then how long would I need to suffer the indignation of putting out the shit that we were presently serving up. "A year," I had been told by one of the other cooks. *"A whole bloody year?"* I had screamed back at him. I just couldn't see myself doing this for a year, and as much respect as I had for my friends, I started admiring them even more for being able to see into the future, but unfortunately, it was not for me and so had decided to cut my losses and head back to the UK.

I had heard that as a student (and I considered myself still to be one as I had only left college approximately two months earlier), one could buy a cheap fight back to the UK for twenty-seven quid and this is what I had planned to do. Then Español said to me, "But what about your passport, you have to get it back from the police, no?"

To which I replied, "No, I have my passport in my bag back at the dorm."

"Jesus Christ!" exclaimed Wolfe. "You mean to tell me you still did not hand your passport into the police station?"

"No," I replied with a look of confusion on my face.

"Then we had better get you out of the city as by now the police will be looking for you."

How the hell was I to know that every new employee that came to work in Switzerland had to hand their passport in to the police?

And now I had made a best friend in the chef, maybe they had a point.

So we set a plan into place that being that they would go to work the next day telling whoever would ask that I had come down with some sort of flu bug and that I was going to be off work for at least a day. Wolfe was going to buy me a ticket to the UK with hopefully the assistance of my student union card, and I was going to Basle for the day. I just needed to get to the Bahnhof at the crack of dawn to get the first train that according to the timetable in the staff cafeteria, departed at 5:45 a.m. Frenchie was going to come with me so that we could by me a ticket unheeded. I was going to hide in the washroom until Frenchie had the ticket and then he was going to hand it to me just as the train was due to depart. On my return later that evening, Wolfe was going to meet me from the station and then all being well, we would go back to the dorm and I would fly out the following morning. "If only it could be that simple," I kept saying to myself, and of course it was not.

Español had suggested I take my passport with me as quite often the police would board the trains and conduct random inspections. I thanked him for his advice and then thought to myself, *What an idiot! Here I was, a wanted man in a foreign country and I am going to leave my passport at the dorm. No way, mate!*

We all woke at 4:00 a.m. and after having conducted our ablutions headed to the train station where upon the plan went into place and the train pulled out of the station at 5:45 a.m. on the dot. *Typical Swiss efficiency*, I thought to myself.

The train journey I had embarked upon I would remember until today as once leaving the city, the world changed from the clean and cosmopolitan style of old and new buildings to an almost immediate transformation, literally after having turned a bend to what I can only describe as a scene out of the *The Sound of Music*. There were Swiss chalets all over the one side of the mountain that were adorned with the most colorful window baskets. The actual hillsides were a lush green that had cows doted all over the place, trimming the grass as they moved around (trying as hard as I might, I just could see a sign of a poop anywhere). *Probably these Swiss people hire someone to go out on an hourly basis, ha!* I thought to myself. It was almost as if

I could have seen Julie Andrews and that Von Trapp twit running down the mountain followed by all those kids.

These spectacular views continued until we were almost into Baslea journey that took me approximately an hour and twenty minutes, if I am not mistaken. It was most certainly a trip I would recommend to anybody.

As I disembarked from the train, I noticed a kiosk that was selling tickets for a daily bus tour that would "guarantee" to please me and would plan stops along the way, along with a lunch stop and one of the local pubs and would have me back by 3:00 p.m., which gave me plenty of time to catch my homeward bound train that I was sure was going to leave at 4:00 p.m. sharp.

As I boarded the bus, I headed for the upper, open air deck where I had heard some English voices, and there and behold, sat two of the most unfortunate-looking young ladies I had ever had the misfortune to see. It took me all of my might not to turn around to the rest of the passengers and exclaim, "No, no, no, they're not all like this in England, believe me when I tell you, we have some pretty ones also." But remembered what my Mum had told me that "Beauty is as beauty does." *But, Mum, I could hear myself thinking, these two look as if they had fallen out of the tallest* ugly tree *the world has ever seen* and *had hit every branch on the way down, before landing in their faces as they hit the bottom.*

As it turned out, my Mum was right again, and for what they missed in good looks, they had certainly made up in character as well as good humor; and have to admit, made the day the most enjoyable I had experienced in a long time.

The bus tour was amazing and we meandered through the fairly mature side of the city streets that were so clean. The flower baskets that hung from each and every lamp post and were kept in absolute pristine condition.

As the tour operator had promised us on booking our tickets, we had stopped at a quaint little bar up the mountain, just outside of Basle where the girls got absolutely plastered and the journey back to the train station was nothing short of a riot. The entire bus had turned into a new "dimension" as my two new English friends had us in stitches from singing some old London Cockney songs to some of the raucous rugby songs.

In any event, a good time was had by all—nobody was sick, not even the girls—but then, I had put this down to the fact that if you were as ugly as they were, probably getting absolutely shit faced at any opportunity was possibly one's best defense, and so practice had been made perfect when it came to drinking copious amounts of beer and the ability of being able keep it all down.

Again as promised, we had arrived in a typical Swiss timely fashion and I wished our entire bus people farewell and boarded the train to Zürich.

I think it was the beer as well as the laughter that had taken its toll and so I sat in my assigned seat and proceeded to nod off. As the train pulled out of the station, the sudden jolt had woken me and what I saw before me was incredible. It was the old mountain goat who had held my knee whilst traveling on the tram from the airport to the Bahnhof. "What were the chances?" I kept saying to myself. Obviously, better than I had given fate credit for!

So I sat there, pretending to be sleeping, despite needing the bathroom, and my eyeballs almost floating around inside my head due to the large quantities of beer I had consumed earlier, but somehow, managed to make it all the way to Zurich; and as soon as the train had come to a stop, got out of my chair, off the train and started bolting toward the nearest washroom with so much determination, I had completely missed Wolfe, who as planned was there to meet me. All I heard was, "Tony, Tony, we have to talk now!"

I said, "Okay, but it will have to be in the washroom as I am just about to pee myself."

The relief was as magnificent as I stood there for what seemed like a lifetime, just emptying my bladder, something I would not be able to manage to hold off from contemplating these days given my *condition*.

Wolfe stood beside me as if pretending to take a pee and then said to me, "The police were at the dorm looking for you this afternoon. Apparently the chef didn't take too kindly to your decapitating his Mouse yesterday, in what he is calling a 'typical English, public execution' and so you cannot stay at the dorm tonight, but I have found a place for you to spend the night tonight before your flight departure tomorrow morning. Here is your ticket for the 8:05 a.m. flight into Heathrow. Come on, let's go," he said in a very urgent manner. I almost said to him, "Sure thing, Batman," but thought better of it as I needed him now more than ever before.

We ran out of the Bahnhof as if we had just robbed a bank, and into a taxi that was waiting by the taxi stand. As I recall the look on the taxi driver's face, I can remember thinking to myself how suspicious we had looked so much so I was surprised he even let us into his cab in the first place. Then Wolfe shouted to him some address and we sped off to my next destination.

It took us approximately five minutes to reach the apartment building. We both jumped out of the car and ran up the steps to this swanky looking building; he pressed a buzzer and women answered it. I started thinking things were looking up.

The door unlocked itself and we both walked in and took the elevator to the fifth floor. As we walked into the apartment, I couldn't help notice the fine quality furniture and the somewhat familiar smell of fragrance. Where had I smelled that perfume before? And then it all fell into place as she walked into the lounge area. Yes, it was

Beatrice. She put her hand forward to shake mine with a beautiful smile saying, "Welcome, Tony, you will be safe here." Wolfe left after about ten minutes as he was required to work overtime at the Bahnhof. She kissed him gently on the cheek and he said to her. "See you later and, please take care of my friend."

We sat on the couch and talked about nothing in particular, and then we watched a bit of TV then polished of a bottle of red wine between the two of us. I could feel my eyes drooping as the wine took effect and decided to take a shower and get an early night as I had to be up early in the morning. I said good night to Beatrice and so desperately wanted to kiss her but then reminded myself that this was my friend's girlfriend, and if it wasn't for him, I would have been a great deal of trouble. I entered the shower and stood there for approximately fifteen minutes letting the hot water wash away my worries.

This time tomorrow I would be back in the UK and sitting down to one of my Mum's specialties.

I got out of the shower, dried myself placed the bathrobe that Beatrice had lent me, fastened it up securely and walked from the washroom to the bedroom that I had been assigned, got into the double bed, lay my head on the pillow, and fell fast asleep.

I awoke to find Beatrice lying beside me, completely naked; I opened my eyes fully and started to say, "But this is wrong." She kissed me long and hard and then said to me, "Wolfe asked me to take care of you, no?"

I thought about what she had said for about a second and half and replied, "Oh okay, go on then."

CHAPTER SEVEN

Homeward Bound

WE HAD ARRIVED AT THE airport at 6:00 a.m. which would have been in plenty of time for my 8:05 a.m. flight via Swiss Air from Zürich to Heathrow, London. We had said our final good-byes and I even got a peck on the cheek from Beatrice. Boy, this lady was hot and I had just managed to kick her out of my bed within two minutes of Wolfe arriving home after his overtime shift at the "office." I was absolutely exhausted after what must have been almost three hours of mad, passionate lovemaking.

A personal record for me, even as I near the ripe old age of fifty-seven, has it yet to be broken (nor will it likely ever be!).

I boarded the flight and sat in my seat with what I could have imagined would only have been described as a pensive look on my face.

As we took off, I tried to recount all that had happened within the last week. It was almost as if I had lived an entire life within that week from my arrival to the long night of passion last night. I mused at the mouse incident to the two English girls I had met yesterday to Frenchie's two psychedelic yawns on the night of my arrival.

Nothing seemed to relate to any sense of order, except that I was leaving Switzerland and some good friends. I started to wonder if I had given it my best shot. Who could possibly tell or would know until the future would unfold and the one day I would say to myself, "You did the right thing by leaving when you did."

One thing is for sure and that is at the age of fifty-seven and someone who was forced into semiretirement as a result of my *condition,* I still to this day am not sure if I made the right move by throwing in the towel when I did. All I can say is that it seemed to be the right decision at the time, and since I am a man who lives by his own convictions, have a sense closure and have to also admit that now I have written about it can most certainly put it at rest in the back of my mind, or can I because . . . what if?

CHAPTER EIGHT

Back to Square One

SO MUM WAS DELIGHTED TO see me (as mums are when their little soldiers come home from battle) and Dad, hmm . . . had what could only be described as a look of disdain on his face that kind of spelled the message "Don't get too comfortable, my boy, as I have a huge shock in store for you." And he was right too.

After approximately two weeks of Mum's exquisite home cooking, my dad had found me another car that had been dropped off at the yard and all it was going cost me was one hundred quid. This time it was a light blue Austin 1100 circa 1967 and was in great shape, so I lapped it up, only to be told the next day that, "Okay, now you have a nice little car, I want you to get in it and drive to wherever you want and don't come back until you've found a job."

I thought to myself, *Bournemouth looks nice this time of the year*, and so headed off to Bournemouth with a sense of adventure in the air and the hope of securing employment, which in fact I did (much to my surprise), but what a dump and a half it was too! I started the same day as securing the position only to be told that I would be sharing a bed with an additional guy who worked the midnight or graveyard shift, which meant that he slept in the bed during the daytime (with his girlfriend) and I would sleep in the same bed during the night time.

Once I saw the living quarters, I had decided this was not for me; and so whilst in Bournemouth, given that it was going to cost me a whole bunch of money to drive home, I had decided to look for additional employment. And so I walked into a hotel that was called back then The Palace Court Hotel. I can remember sitting in the lobby waiting for the food and beverage manager to come and meet me for an interview. I sat there for at least an hour, watching the hotel guests checking in and out, wondering if I would ever be fortunate enough to be part of what looked like to me to be a well-oiled machine and not even appreciating that this next adventure would change my life forever.

I was interviewed by the food and beverage manager and then by the executive chef, a huge man in height by the name of Michael Burr. I had been successful in being granted a position as a commis chef. This position is basically one step up from being a trainee and used to be considered the entry level into the real world within the culinary system.

I started work the next day and can remember my living quarters being a small room, no larger than a large storage cupboard, but it was adequate and would have to suffice until something became available in the staff accommodation behind the hotel but still attached to the building. I had started my shift at 8:00 a.m. and felt as if I was literally the youngest kid that had ever walked into the kitchen. At the age of eighteen my friend Robin couldn't believe I had completed college; I looked so young. I also felt as if I was going to be fair play for some of the waitresses who had taken and interest in my youthful appearance.

It was my first day in the cold kitchen working with an ancient Turkish guy who, was for me, the dirtiest, rudest old man one could ever wish to meet. His comments to the female staff were atrocious and the chef seemed powerless to do anything about it because he was only part time and was the cheapest chef on the market. As time progressed, I came to understand that in fact, he (Charlie) could be one of the funniest guys around and so everybody took everything he said with a pinch of salt. I worked a second day and then a third day in his area to find out that the fourth day, I would be working this section on my own. I didn't sleep a wink that night fearing the next day. I came into work to find all the prep work I had done the day before had disappeared. What was I to do, go and complain to the chef or just get on with it? My new friend Robin came over to see me. He was a good-looking guy and certainly had a way with the ladies and was the hotel's apprentice. Sensing the panic in my movements, he came over to see if I was okay to which I replied, "No, I don't think so."

"Why?" said Robin. "Has all your *mise en place* (preparation) gone?"

"Yes," I said to Robin, "I can't understand where it has all gone. I mean, I stayed behind an extra two hours last night making sure I was in good shape for today."

"What time did you leave the kitchen last night?"

"I locked the gate at 10:00 p.m.," was my honest reply.

"Ah," said Robin, "Charlie has a set of keys to the kitchen and to make himself look good and indispensable, probably came in after you left and threw all of your prep work away. He does it to every new person who starts work here."

"Asshole," I said. And with that, Robin picked up his knife and said to me, "Okay, Chef, where do we start?" And with this I gave him a list of things we needed to prep for the buffet.

We had it all prepared with, I would suggest, barely two minutes to go before service would start. That night, I was so exhausted I had decided that I was going to fix Charlie and so left the walk-in chiller in an awful mess. *Big* mistake.

I came to work that next day and got the biggest bollocking of my life. Charlie was throwing stuff out of the walk-in and shouting, "Mike (the chef's name), come and look at the mess this littley bastard Tom has left for me today." I hated it when people got my name wrong, how hard was it to remember my name. "Tony," I said to Charlie as I walked up to him. Another *big* mistake. "Tom, you littley bastard, what the hell are you playing at?" I said to him, "The same as you were playing the night before last." And yet the *biggest* mistake so far was just as soon as I had walked away from him, as true as I am sitting here typing this, the largest kitchen knife I had ever seen whisked its way within a foot of my head. Yes, this old bastard had almost killed me with his butcher's knife. I looked at him and saw that he hadn't yet put his teeth in, or hopefully (and better still) he had swallowed them and was choking on them. I looked at him again and smiled at him and said, "You missed, you miserable old git."

The chase was on, him with a small vegetable preparation knife and me with a rolling pin I had been given as I ran passed the pastry chef (Barry Earl was his name). Charlie was wearing the hotel standard offering of footwear and I, a pair of runners (there weren't enough of the standard footwear for me upon my joining this culinary mad house) and I definitely had the advantage. I ran out of the pastry area (complete with rolling pin), passed the chef's office (a quick glance confirmed that he had left) into the sauce section and around the stove into the *entremetier* (vegetable) section. I stood there waiting for him to arrive in the sauce section. He finally arrived, huffing and puffing like the old fart that he was, and then he threw his little vegetable knife at me and missed me by a mile. I then imitated his old fart look by covering my teeth with my lips (hopefully looking as if I had no teeth) and taunted him by saying, with the slightest whistle with my teeth, "You missed me, you old bastard," and with this I made haste to the cold kitchen, around the prep table that was in the middle of the prep area and waited for him again. He arrived with a carving knife, his eyes bulging with anger. He could see that I was starting to enjoy the pursuit and after shaking my rolling pin and then giving him the middle finger, made my way back to the pastry area where Barry and Robin were now cheering me on. As I arrived at the wooden pastry table, I heard a thud. *Yes!* I thought to myself and true enough, Charlie's standard hotel footwear, along with a piece of lettuce that he had thrown out earlier in anger, had justifiably joined forces to bring this mad-eyed, huffing and puffing, toothless wonder's chase to a halt. A cheer went out in the kitchen as Charlie lay on the ground, holding onto his face screaming, "Mike, Mike, that littley Tom just hit me."

"You lying old bastard!" I shouted as I walked over to him. He had caught the side of his head on the corner of the table and he wasn't bleeding but looked as if he was going to cultivate a beautiful shiner. I looked down at him and said, "Does it hurt, Charlie?" To which he replied, "Of course it does, you stupid littley schmuck."

All I said was, "You mean 'little' don't you, you stupid bug-eyed old bastard, and good bloody job because next time your balls come off." At that moment the chef walked into the kitchen saw what had happened and off Charlie went again. "Mike, Mike, look what that littley bastard Tom has done." The chef looked at Barry who then proceeded to shake his head from side to side as if to say "no way," to which the chef responded to Charlie, "Get up and get to work or else sod off home!" It was obvious that Barry had been held high in the chef's books as his reaction to Charlie's whining had shown that chef knew exactly what Charlie was like. It was such a pleasure watching Charlie drag himself to his feet, holding onto his face that had in the short amount of time, swollen up to the size of a golf ball and was starting to go blue.

I looked at him and said, "My name is Tony not Tom," and with this grabbed my balls as a reminder as to what I had in my mind for him he the next time he were to try anything.

Needless to say that after such an event, I didn't have any further issues with Charlie, but sad to say, he couldn't get to call me Tony and Tom; it was right up until the last day, when by which time, everybody was calling me Tom—even me!

CHAPTER 9

The Day the World Lost Barry Earl

BARRY WAS VERY MUCH LIKE a big brother to Robin and I. He was thirty-four years old and was married to a beautiful lady who was twenty-six. Barry used to come to work and joke about the neighbors and how they would complain about their noisy lovemaking. He was a real mate and we all loved him (well, everyone except Charlie). The new guy in the pot wash area was a guy by the name of Tommy, a Scottish guy who was no taller than five foot two inches tall, if he was an inch. This guy just loved to fight. I remember one night Robin and I were out with a couple of girls from Sweden.

Mine was a five and his was a ten and what a beauty she was too. She used to wear a white cheesecloth dress without any underwear on and it didn't leave much to the imagination. Mine on the other hand was dressed as if she was about to take a trek up Mount Everest, which is why, had we been alone (without Robin) we would have been fine. In any event, what transpired that night I suppose should have been predicted because after a few drinks, Robin would get fairly aggressive (whereas all I ever wanted to do was go around a kiss everybody), and this particular night, there were a whole bunch of blokes in this nightclub and they had their eyes on Robin's girl. Well this upset him no end so he decided to give one of them the finger. The only trouble with this was that they (*all* five of them) were looking at his girl at the same time. To cut a long story short, we both showed up at work the next day with bruises on our faces, except that Robin was far worse than I was because on getting whacked the first time, I had decided to stay down in the bush that I had landed in, whereas Robin felt compelled to carry on.

On inspection of the damage, Tommy and Barry decided we would all be going back the next night with our girlfriends and again sit in the same spot we had sat in last night except it would be me that would give the finger and Tommy and Barry would follow us out and assist us if need be should there be any problems.

So the stage was set, we were all in our specific positions when all five guys came into the club looking somewhat the worse for wear, which meant one of two things. Either we had done a better job than we had originally given ourselves credit for, or else they had been given a "good hiding" by some others, after us. I felt it was the latter but when Barry saw the state of them as they walked in, he gave us both the two thumbs up and kind of sniggered. At this point I had decided that no matter who was responsible for these guys' messy faces, that as long as Barry thought we had done it to them, this was good enough for me.

They started looking at Robin's girl again and I gave them the finger and one of the cheeky bastards starting laughing at me. I felt like saying to him, "Well, she may not be as beautiful as his but it's a lot more than you have hanging off your arm, you ugly twat!" And with that gave them all the Italian gesture for "F you."

Well you should have seen what happened next. As they lunged for us (there was about ten feet between us and the bar) from the right side of me, Tommy came out like a lion ready to kill and Barry was right behind him. I have to admit I have never until today seen a short little guy like Tommy hit with so much accuracy and with so much force that the sound of fist against the face was pretty sickening. In less than ten seconds it was all over; the first two that Tommy had hit were out cold and the other three (one of which was Tommy's, and the other two were Barry's) were in no fit state to carry on, and the beauty of it all was the fact that Robin and I didn't have to lift a finger and watched it all from ringside seats!

On the way home we all laughed at how people would have paid a small fortune to have sat in the same seats that we had sat in night tonight, if in fact it had been a scheduled bout and how Tommy and Barry were only putting the final touches on our handy work of the night before (yeah right, Bazzer).

It's because of comradely such as this that makes it very hard for me to write the next few paragraphs.

Each Wednesday, we would go to the rounder's park in between split shifts. It was a leisurely twenty-minute casual jaunt from the hotel and Bournemouth being Bournemouth, a seaside resort area on the south coast of England, the weather was almost great most of the time and today was no exception. As Robin and I headed the pack toward the field, Barry was bringing up the rear with most of the pretty waitresses (along with the mixture of the not so pretty ones) and we headed for the diamond and was practicing our batting skills when Karl, our new sous chef, showed up on his brand new Yamaha 750cc motorbike. This stopped all the practicing and we all went look at this bright, shiny yellow-and-red beast. It was a very cool-looking machine.

All the girls were crowding round and stroking it as if it was a tiger. Then Karl asked me if I would like a ride on it; the fastest thing I had ever been on before was a Honda 50 (or what we used to call a "Nifty 50") and I reluctantly said that I would. I was putting on my crash helmet when Barry came over to me and said, "Hey, little brother, make sure that helmet is fastened properly." And he proceeded to fasten the straps and adjust them so that the helmet sat securely on my head. Feeling as safe as houses, I cautiously pulled and opened up the throttle and this thing shot away like no tomorrow. In fact, I had probably only gone approximately two hundred yards and decided I had had enough, gingerly turned the bike around, paying extra attention to the weight of the machine so as not to drop it, and then very cautiously drove it back to where Karl and Barry, as well as all the girls were standing. I got off the bike realizing that I had not impressed anybody and handed the helmet back to Karl thinking to myself, *Well at least you're still in one piece.*

Then Karl asked Barry if he wanted a turn. Barry accepted the offer, and placed the helmet on his head started up the bike and before I could say, "Hey, brother, make sure your helmet is fastened properly," he was off like a bat out of hell.

What happened next was beyond belief!

The road we were riding the bike on was particularly narrow and had trees that were an average of twelve feet apart. The road surface itself had a very rough and sharp granite-like covering. Barry had decided to show off to the girls and had opened the throttle to the point that he was speeding so fast he had lost control of the bike, and on swerving to avoid an oncoming vehicle, had hit the first tree and then hit the second tree without his helmet on, and had bounced off the second tree that elevated him to about twenty feet and then landed in the exact middle of the road. All I saw was, after hearing the revving of the engine, a crash helmet flying through the air and then Barry's body being propelled from the second tree, and then seeing his head hit the ground. It was the most sickening thing I had ever seen.

I screamed at the top of my voice, "Barry's had an accident!" And I started to run over to where he lay which was about one hundred and fifty yards from where I stood. Then I noticed my run had changed into a walk as I saw some girls running toward me with their hands over their mouths screaming, "Tony, don't go there—it's awful!" I froze for a second and thought to myself, *How can you not go there, he's practically your brother?* Then I walked briskly dreading what I was going to find once I had reached him.

What I saw brought an instant cry of fear.

Barry had always been a beach bum and had always sported a beautiful tan. But what I saw brought horror to my face. His typically brown face was an ashen white apart from the four trails of thick scarlet blood that ran from both ears and nostrils.

I couldn't see the wound that must have been gapping from the underside of his head, but knew it must have been there for the two trails of thick, glistening, scarlet red blood that ran evenly down either side of him toward the gutters were too much to be coming from his ears and nose. I knelt down beside him and said, "Barry, it's going to be all right mate." As I said this, a huge eruption of blood the same color as was pouring out of his ears and nose started pouring out his mouth. Of course, I knew it was over for Barry and on anticipating the nature of his wounds took comfort in the fact that it had probably been a relatively quick demise.

I didn't even hear the ambulance pull up but I can still remember one of the ambulance guys saying to me, "It's okay, mate, we'll take it from here." I sat on the side of the road as they lifted Barry's lifeless body onto the stretcher. I can remember asking what seemed to be a pointless question, "Which hospital are you taking him to?" The answer I should have expected but for the life of me did not. "Is he a personal friend of yours?" the ambulance guy had asked. "More like a brother," was my reply as I stood at the ambulance as they closed the doors.

"Well, I'm very sorry but your brother is going straight to the Bournemouth morgue."

This was the day the world had lost Barry Earl.

I sat beside the road not knowing what to do next. The ambulance guy was washing down the road in an effort to dispose of Barry's blood. He came over to me and asked if I was going to be okay. "What choice do I have?" I had whispered to myself. Robin came out of nowhere and I said to him, "Do you know where the chef lives, he has to know about this and now."

Robin had been to the chef's house on one occasion before and said he knew where it was. I rang the bell and we waited and waited, then I rang the bell again. Then I started to think about how I should I break the news to the chef—that one of the people within the profession that he had respected so much—had passed on.

The door opened and there stood the chef. "Barry's dead, Chef." He went white and said, "Okay, boys, thanks for the news. Tony, you will have to work the pastry department tonight."

"Yes, Chef," was all I could say.

CHAPTER TEN

The Worst Shift You Could Ask a Man to Cover

I ARRIVED BACK THE HOTEL; I called my mum to let her know what had happened. Typically, whilst living in Bournemouth, I only went home after each ten days. I had an arrangement with the chef that I would work ten days straight, and then take my two sets of two days off together. This would work most weeks because had the four of us had been fighting; I would avoid going home to face the questions as to why I had a black eye or a cut lip. Don't get me wrong, I had not turned into a rebel or a troublemaker, but more of a young lad establishing his mark in life as a man. Which I have come to appreciate more as my men are growing older, and I have to admit that each time I see Chris (my eldest son) get into a fight at hockey and hear about some asshole take a swing at Dan (my youngest of the two) and knocks him out for no apparent reason, it sickens me to the stomach.

I have to tell you about a floor hockey game that Chris, Dan and their buddies were playing at the John Braithwaite Community Centre here in North Vancouver. Michelle (my daughter) had shown up with a friend and we were watching this game and a guy looked as if he had it in for Chris as to be fair, Chris is a very good and fair player.

To cut a long story short, this guy got into a tussle with Chris and pulled a right that was going to connect with Chris's jawbone and on discussing the action later, Chris had admitted seeing it coming and ducked. In any event the perpetrator had been evicted from the game and as he walked passed myself and Michelle, I whispered,

"You bloody asshole." And as I felt myself moving toward him, I heard Michelle, as if she was addressing the dog, say with all the authority of a dog owner, "Leave it, Dad, leave it!"

The point I am trying to make here is that no matter what happens to you or your friends and family, there is a bond that keeps you whole, not necessarily as one, but pretty damn close.

Now I am certainly not a believer in ghosts, whereas my beautiful wife, who hails from Indonesia, believes quite the contrary; and yet, as I tried to enter that kitchen, felt as if Barry was already there. I sat in the chef's office for what I thought was going to be a few seconds and what turned out be over ten minutes.

A few of the waiters had come by to offer their condolences and despite the two teams (the culinary as well as the service) usually hating each other's guts, for some reason these guys were very different, and their well wishes were all very sincere. They all appreciated that we, as a hotel, had lost a very dear friend and that the team would not be the same as a result. I got out of the chef's chair and started walking toward the pastry area and there, as if a reminder of our friendship, was the rolling pin that he had passed to me during my conflict with Charlie.

My eyes started to well up with tears but I fought them back. Charlie Boy, on the other hand, came into the kitchen and threw his arms around me and starting sobbing like a blithering idiot and was slobbering all over me, like a bulldog that was trying to negotiate the consumption of a couple of live wasps.

He had been drinking quite heavily by the smell of his breath and started to slur his words. I grabbed him by the throat and said to him, "Now listen to me, you useless old fart, I have lost a best friend today and now have the task of covering for him and—look at me, you son of a bitch—I cannot possibly cover for you at the same time, so you go to your section and you had better do a damn good job because if you don't, Charlie my boy, you will be going home *without your balls*! Now do we understand one another?" He shook his head as if to say yes. I let go of his throat and pushed him to one side. He stumbled for a bit and then regained his balance.

I think looking back at this incident, should probably have thanked Charlie for being there when he was because it allowed me to disperse a lot of the pent up anger that I had as a result of the day's events but had I done so, would never have heard the end of it.

Service was busy that night and in addition to this, I was able to royally bugger up twelve Bavarian flans as well as thirty-six crème caramels.

That night, Charlie Boy had managed to sober up sufficiently to carry out his end of the service to some level of satisfactory. I think the service staff had been very tolerant of us all. I know for a fact that I had ballsed up a few orders and not a word was uttered.

As Charlie Boy left the kitchen, he looked at me and said with so much sincerity in his voice, "Good night, Tom."

I guess he had tried to remember my name but maybe also, down in his heart, he was missing Barry in his own way, and I respected this; but where on earth had he got the name "Tom" from—I mean, how hard was it to remember the name Tony?

Some things were just unexplainable, I thought to myself, *Just like why had Barry been taken from us at such an early age?*

Good grief, did I have some learning to do, not the least of which was how to grieve in a mature and dignified manner.

That night I sobbed my heart out and knew that I had woken most of the female residents or visitors, and I could hear one of them say, "Maybe we should go in there and see if he is all right?"

To which I heard one of the servers by the name of Gary say, "Nah, leave him alone, let him get it out of his system, if I know Tom, he will be as good a gold in the morning."

Good grief, if I hear that name one more time, I am going to kill someone, but it can wait until the morning

I woke still in my clothes that were sopping wet with perspiration, had this whole thing with Barry been a nasty nightmare or had it actually happened? My throat was dry and on observing myself in the mirror, it appeared as if I had been dragged through a hedge backward. *Oh well,* I thought to myself, *another day, another dollar.* I dressed myself in my bathrobe and headed for the showers that were just down the hallway.

There were two, as one might expect—one for each gender and depending who was staying overnight; it was a bit of a hit and a miss as to which one you got to use. But this particular morning both were empty, which was a bit of a bonus as it meant I didn't have to witness any boobs or bottoms of the "overnighters" as they would scurry from the shower into the residents room. I mean some of them were very shapely whereas others were a tad "well-covered" as my Mum would used to stay.

I envied Barry living out as he had some sort of normality in his life. Something about that comment didn't feel right; I chose to ignore the uncomfortable feeling and carried on with washing my "bits." As I exited the shower, a female waitress by the name of Sandra sat in the hallway almost naked (apart from her knickers and bra) sobbing her heart out. I wanted to say something but chose not to as if she had had a fight with her boyfriend, it was no business of mine, and then just as I was passing her she lunged at me with a heartfelt sob saying, "I am so sorry." I hugged her and said, "It's all right." Then the penny had finally dropped, she was crying because of Barry and so it wasn't a bad dream after all. What had I been thinking whilst in the shower? Oh my goodness, why hadn't I been able to tell Barry to fasten up his helmet as he had been able to do for me? I started to cry with Sandra and we went into her room due to its close proximity, laid on the bed, and fell asleep in her arms.

It was 10:00 a.m. when I woke up with shock—shit, I was an hour late for work and the chef was going to be as mad as hell. As I got to Sandra's door, I saw a note with name of Tony written on the front of the page that had been folded in two. I opened it and what was written inside brought yet another flood of tears. It was from the chef and it read, "Great job last night and yesterday, take the rest of the day off. Thank you for everything. Mike."

I mean he had actually signed it Mike, not Executive Chef Burr, but Mike. What a guy this guy was? Mike. I lay in bed all day with Sandra and all we did was hold each other.

If only I knew then what I know today! (It makes me want to spit.)

The phone rang in the corridor and someone shouted, "It's for you, Tony." I picked up the phone and almost gagged on the stench of cigarettes that came from the mouthpiece "Hello, Tony, this is Peter from here in Storrington."

"Yes, Mr. Peter," I replied somewhat confused, "what can I do for you?"

"Well, Tony, you remember our Chef Justine, well he has decided to move on and Daphne and I were so impressed with you while you were with us here in the summer months of last year that we were wondering if you would like to join us here as our chef?" I calmly said to him that I would certainly think about it and would get back to him after the weekend.

Well what a turn up for the books. I had just been offered the head chef's job in what I considered to be one of the best restaurants in the south of England.

Peter was a retired engineer who, along with a man by the name of Mr. Russell, had been the first two gentlemen to invent the automatic kettle under the company name of "Russell and Hobbs." This kettle would turn itself off as it reached boiling point. It was considered to be quite the technological breakthrough back then.

He had purchased this two-story cottage and had converted it into a small bar and restaurant that had thirty-three seats only that were downstairs with very comfortable living quarters upstairs. The gardens were very functional that had a wrought iron gated area at the side of the cottage with an arched brick wall and a grape vine growing all over the entire construction. I would like to think it was your typical English countryside rose garden that has a generous portion of it laid out for fresh herbs. The kitchen itself was a culinary dream—its layout with beautiful paned glass windows along the half side of the entire building that lent itself to all the natural daylight that was available. I would have imagined the property would have been late eighteenth century and yet everything inside of it was brand new. A dream of a property and they wanted me for their head chef!

What a delightful proposition, I had thought to myself, *but could I do the job?*

"Well, obviously they think you can," came back the answer from Dad, whom I always consulted with major career decisions such as these, and the advantage I had with this particular situation was that Dad knew the property as he had found me the summer job in the first place by reading some back copies of the *Caterer and Hotelkeeper* and then by dropping me off there for my original interview. "I tell you what, think about it over the weekend and then call him back on Monday and let him know, but remember one thing, it is your decision and whatever you decide, we are behind you one hundred percent."

I went to see Barry at his grave site. Had it been a month already since we had laid him to rest? I would never forget that day as it was the very first funeral I had ever attended and it was a burial. I could not understand how a burial could be so final. I had had the honor of standing by Christine, his wife, as they lowered the casket into the ground and hugged her as she sobbed so uncontrollably. My heart broke for her.

It was cold day, the day I had decided to go for my chat with "Bazzer." I had also thought it would be nice to take some fresh flowers and decided to walk all the way from the hotel to his grave site, which took me approximately an hour and a half. Upon arriving, I had forgotten where exactly he had been buried so I spent an additional twenty-five minutes trying to figure out where it was, but on finding it, knew instantly it was Barry's. Firstly because it was new and also, I had thought how classy his headstone had looked with the majority of it being of the highly polished black granite with a two foot square etched area with the words in the raised and polished form as the rest of the tombstone:

> Here lies Barry John Earl loving husband to Christine Nicola Earl and a dear friend to so many January 6th 1939 to September 26th 1974. May God forever hold you in his arms.

I placed the flowers up against his tombstone as the ceramic that was provided there, had been recently filled with some fresh Lilly of the Valley. *My Mum's favorite,* I had thought to myself.

I started off by telling him how much I missed him and how Charlie had finally got fired for throwing that knife at me a week before his terrible accident.

"I had actually pleaded on his behalf," I said to Barry. "But the GM was having nothing to do with it and had told the employment tribunal that since you had passed away as a result of a motorbike accident that he couldn't afford to lose anybody else from his brigade and so considered Charlie a liability and that he should be locked up forever, and the keys thrown away!"

It was as if I could hear Barry laughing his head off. Then I started on the job offer and as I said to him, "So what do you think, Bazzer?" I felt a warm hand being placed into mine as Christine said, "Listen to what he has to say, Tony, he would often tell me how much he loved and respected you, and feel sure the advice he will give today will be good and sound." I squeezed her hand without looking at her and said, "Did you hear everything I said to Barry?" To which she replied, "Yes. I also heard Barry laughing at the story you told about Charlie."

"You too?" I said as I turned to look at her.

"Honestly, Tony."

I could feel a tear run down my cheek as I said to her, "I'm sorry but I miss him so much."

"We all do, Tony, we all do."

"Well, I really should be getting back to work now so please stay in touch." I let go of her hand, turned, and started walking back to the hotel and until today have not seen or heard from her since.

So I had made the decision. Couldn't honestly tell you whether or not I had had a conversation with Barry on the topic, but knew in my heart that I had to take the opportunity and give it my best shot.

The next day I was in the chef's office with my decision.

"Have you spoken to anyone with regards to this decision?"

I very comfortably said, "Yes, Chef, my Dad and Barry."

My farewell do was the typical kitchen celebration, although not quite as drastic as Dave's had been at the Masonic lodge, where you were coated in the worst bucket of stinkiest shit that they could put together, then fill you full of beer and then cart you off to your room. Although this particular time, I had an old Turkish fart looking out for me. Yes, Charlie Boy.

I had been to see the GM to thank him for his kindness in dealing with the issue of Charlie and his attempted murder of me and explained that it really wasn't all his fault. (Why? I had no idea as it seemed pretty real at the time.)

Now knowing that the chef was going to be even more in the shit after having given my notice and having Charlie sign a declaration stating that if ever he were ever to try and assassinate a colleague again, he'd agree that he would go for a psychiatric evaluation; the GM had agreed to reinstate Charlie Boy.

I really didn't need Charlie Boy looking after me as I hadn't had that much to drink but for the sake of allowing him to gain a little respect, went along with him. Had I known he was going to sit me down in the kitchen after everyone had left, and then pull out bottle of brandy and proceed to get absolutely plastered while telling me his life story, I should have thought better of it but figured I owed it to him.

In fact, I felt quite sorry for Charlie Boy as, by all accounts, he had had quite a rough life.

When I left him in the kitchen, he was nicely wrapped in a bunch of stinky old kitchen rags and a pillow made of the same; he was crying saying, "I love you, Tom . . . I love you, Tom." To which I bleated at him, "It's Tony, you dipstick. Tony is my name." And as I heard him passing out he let out a cackle and said, "You're right, it's Tony."

As I was leaving the next morning for home, I met the chef in the lobby for a scheduled farewell. He and the GM presented me with a carving knife as a parting gift and insisted that I wear my chef's whites for the last time. Chef looked as if he had been up all night—his eyes were so bloodshot.

We said our good-byes and then I went to my room to change into my regular clothes and then walked around the back of the hotel to get into my car where I met Tommy, who hugged me and announced to me that this morning, Charlie Boy had been found dead on the kitchen floor of a heart attack, possibly brought on by alcoholic blood poisoning.

I had decided there and then that it was time for me to leave. I shook Tommy's hand one more time and without saying a word, got into my car and drove home.

CHAPTER ELEVEN

Off to the Sane Part of the World?

I SPENT THE WEEKEND AT Mum and Dad's and then headed down to Storrington the next Monday morning, bright and early. I had thought that Justine would have still been there to greet me but apparently, he and Peter had had a falling out over the weekend and so Justine had decided to cut his losses and depart a week early.

This was no particular big deal for me as the menu hadn't changed within the last year, so all I had to do was jump in and get my hands dirty.

My assistant was a rather large young lady who had just arrived from France after having completed a cordon bleu course in Paris and was the daughter of a friend of Peter's. In any event, she resigned the next day, as according to Daphne, she was desperately in love with Justine. "Well good luck with that one," I had said to myself and as he had admitted to me that he was a homosexual (not that I had any issues with this as I have always been of the opinion "live and let live"), but then I could have been wrong or maybe he had been and had turned the corner and has decided to go straight.

Who knew and who cared? I had a job to do and I was going to give it my best shot, but I needed to find an assistant and fast.

It was as if it had been fate but I would have imagined as if this would have been Peter's and mine because just as Sarah had walked out of the kitchen, in walked Bob Saunders.

"Is the chef around?" he asked, to which I was very proud to be able say, "Yes, I am the chef." Bob had looked a bit surprised to have seen such a "boyish" head chef, he later revealed to me.

We hit it off immediately and as I had done two summers ago, he was able to get his suitcase from the car that his dad had driven him down in.

So there we were, two brand-new lads starting to work in our new restaurant—within just a day of each other.

What I liked about Bob the most, apart from his obvious culinary talents, was his sense of humor. Bob had the ability to find something funny in any desperate situation and to this day, quite often smile at some of the antics we got up to. In no time, we became friends and colleagues rather than chef and assistant, something Peter frowned upon.

I had since found out that Peter had been to a restaurant school in the Midlands for a period of approximately three months, and there had learned how to become a restaurant "patron/manager" which I compared to becoming a head chef after two weeks at a culinary institution.

He was a pompous ass and soon started getting up my nose.

I can remember him calling me into his office complaining about Bob and then saying to me, "Well I am afraid he going to have to go, Tony, as I can see your level of professionalism sliding." And with no further explanation, he walked out of the office. I thought about this for a while and had come to the conclusion that he was perhaps, a bit put out that Bob and I were getting along so well, which obviously went against the grain based on what he had been taught at the restaurant school.

The next day, Peter called me into his office and said to me, "Well?"

"Well what, Peter?"

"Did you tell him?"

"Tell who, what?"

I could see he was starting to get frustrated with my answers.

"Did you tell Bob that he had to leave?"

"Oh that . . . no, Peter, I'm afraid you will have to do that as effective immediately, I am handing in my notice." And with that placed my letter of resignation on his desk right in front of him.

He started waffling on about how I was making a big mistake and that Bob was just an assistant and that I was throwing away the chance of a lifetime—the usual BS that one would expect from someone who thought he knew it all, and yet had been brought to his knees but someone who was fifty years younger than him.

I walked away from him my mind had been made up. Why should I continue to work for some pompous asshole, who couldn't stand the fact that he had a harmonious kitchen team?

The next day Daphne came to discuss the issue with me as "Peter was too upset to come to work." *Ha!* I thought to myself. *What a bloody wimp. One minute he is playing le grand patron, the next minute he is sending his wife down to sort out* his *mess.*

I explained to Daphne what Peter had asked me to do and all she could say was, "This is absolutely preposterous." And with that, she stormed off upstairs to give him, what I would have hoped was, a right bollocking. I still wish I had been a fly on the wall of the bedroom when she spoke to him (although on hindsight, maybe it wasn't that necessary) as from that day forward, he avoided me until the restaurant closed its doors for good, some seven months later. Apparently, after having our little t te-à-t te he had started hitting the booze a little too much and would start insulting the quests—a bit like Basil Fawlty from *Fawlty Towers*—in fact this would best describe Peter to a T. Now why had I not thought of this comparison previously?

Both Bob and I had become good friends with our maître d' or restaurant manager; and given the fact that the restaurant was closing it doors for good, I took Juan's offer of sharing his drive across the English Channel, through France and Spain to his home town of Algeciras, which was located at the southern tip of Spain next to Torremelenos and a couple of hundred kilometers from the rock of Gibraltar.

Bob couldn't come with us; he had just gotten engaged to his girlfriend Kathy, and rightly so, had put her foot down.

There was Juan, myself, and all his belongings, including half of his wife's clothes, stuffed into this dark blue Ford Escort ready to take on the world.

I had planned the route and had presented it to Juan who, with his "Manuel" look (again from the *Fawlty Towers* show) had just said to me, "Si, si, Señor Chef, it look very good."

At this juncture, I should like to point out that the similarities with the employees at the restaurant stop here, and those of you who are familiar with Chef Terry of *Fawlty Towers* will hopefully appreciate this point.

We arrived at Dover, where the customs people took a good look at this little dark blue Ford Escort that was stuffed to the hilt and waved us through. The same thing happened at Calais, our French destination, after a horrendous channel crossing on the hovercraft by the name of "Swift." We drove all way through France without incident and then reached the Basque border, and this is where the brown stuff started to hit the fan. It was pretty cold when we arrived there, and the customs people were the most miserable I had ever met. They took one look at the car and started shouting something at Juan. I was a little unnerved at their aggressiveness and so left all the translation to Juan.

Word was out that there was a shipment of drugs being transported across the border in a dark blue Ford Escort no less. I looked at Juan and said, "Hey, pal, if you have been using me as an accomplice, then there is going to be hell to pay." To which he replied, "I know nothing about what these men are talking about." I felt so much like telling him to cut the "Manuel" bollocks out but would possibly been answered with a "Que?" and just could not have handled it.

We sat inside the customs area as we watched the customs guys just literally empty the car of its contents and spread it over a large expanse of land. When they were satisfied that we were clean, the chief inspector came into the waiting area and said, "He's okay, you can go now."

I looked at Juan and said to him, "Aren't they going to at least help us put this shit back into the car?" He just looked at me and said, "Si . . . I mean no."

We spent the hour and half repacking everything, trying to jam it all back into the car, which ended up being a miracle that it did but this was down to my effort because what I realized was that when Juan had said, "Is full . . . no more . . . we go now," it was my bloody suitcase that wasn't going to fit into the car.

It did, finally, and as a result of my making it fit into the car, Juan had to drive for the next two hours with his head cocked off to one side.

Two hours into driving over the mountains in the Basque region, it had started to snow quite heavily. So much, so that the traffic had come to an absolute standstill as we had tried to negotiate one of the steep mountain highway roads. Drivers who had become inpatient were paying the price by being nudged into ditches by the bigger vehicles. Juan had correctly pointed out that it was my turn to drive and so as we were now stationary with what looked as if nowhere to go, I decided it would only be fair that we changed seats, if only so that I could share the discomfort of having my neck cocked at angle as a result of my insisting (reasonably so, I think) that my suitcase, once again, be part of the original inventory. Upon exiting the vehicle, I had almost shit myself when I had realized how close we were to the edge that looked as if it could have been a two hundred foot drop. "And where were the guard rails? No-bloody-where, that's where."

I settled myself into the driver's side and had noticed it has started to snow quite heavily once again, and on top of this, the wind had picked up to gusts now. I closed my eyes hoping to get some sleep. I had been turning the engine on periodically, in order to warm us up. We had half a tank full of fuel, so I was not concerned about using up as much as it's to keep us warm.

Juan was already asleep and I had dozed off for split second, as if being lullabied by the wind and then woke up with a start as I had felt the car move.

I kept my eyes open and waited for the next gusts, and sure enough, with each gust of wind, we were being blown closer and closer to the rail-less edge. I didn't even bother to wake Juan and just started the engine. As I started to shift the gearstick into first, another gust of wind blew us even closer to the edge. I had to make a move and slowly let the clutch out. At first it had gone well as we inched our way forward but then, with every additional gust, it was as if we were being blown backward again.

Then as if to add insult to injury there was an eighteen wheeler being blown toward us. We were on an incline and so it seemed nothing was going to stop it. I broke all the rules of driving in the snow and just floored the accelerator instantly spinning the wheels. The car responded to a degree as we moved slightly forward away from the precipice, then an additional gust of wind that had strangely come from behind us seemed to help us move forward but even closer to the 18 wheeler that seemed to be on a collision course with us now. Then Juan woke up, "What is happening, Señor Tony?" I said to him in a sarcastic answer, "We are going to die." Then he went on to pray. "Por favor, Jesus Christus . . . blah blah blah."

It was just at the moment the eighteen-wheeler had struck the passenger side of our car, but because I had not let up on the accelerator, the spinning wheels had actually moved us alongside of the truck and so it was the front wheel of this truck that had struck the car. It had knocked us to the left, away from the danger zone, and after this, we arrived at the top of the highway hill and on driving over it saw not one stranded vehicle ahead of us.

Juan was still crossing his chest as we arrived at the crest of the hill and still blabbering away in Spanish to his maker when I said to him, "Juan, it's okay, we are safe now."

"Señor Tony, it is a miracle . . . I love you . . . I love you!"

Then I thought to myself, *First it was Charlie Boy and now you. I really should to start looking for a new career!*

CHAPTER TWELVE

A Month in Spain

AFTER OUR ORDEAL AT THE St. Sebastian border, the night on "Hell's Mountain," and the nonstop drive the length of Spain, a stop off in Madrid (naturally), we arrived at Juan's village of Algeciras at 3:00 p.m. to one of the warmest welcomes I could ever have imagined. There were flags flying and there was a group of Mariachis playing their guitars with such conviction, I was totally in awe of the whole event.

Then Juan's wife appeared from the house in what seemed like a wedding ceremony, surrounded by little girls dressed in similar styled attire, with his Mum and Dad-in-law in tow dressed in what appeared to be their Sunday best. It was almost as if he was being welcomed home like a hero.

His wife was cute but not outstandingly beautiful, as he had described her to me constantly, but then as my mum always said to me, "Beauty is in the eye of the beholder." This was definitely a case of the latter as she had a fairly attractive face with long flowing black hair, but could only have been five foot nothing and had what I would have called a wide birth to her, but do you know what, they looked so happy together, it really didn't matter; they were obviously very much in love with each other and that was good enough for me.

My only real concern was that Juan had said that given I was going to be there for a month, his wife Margareta would introduce me to some of her friends. I only hoped they were taller than she was and that they could hopefully be a bit slimmer.

We ate that night what can only be described as the most sumptuous buffet I had ever laid my eyes upon. There were lobsters and prawns cooked in garlic butter, in cheese sauces, on lemon butter—you name it, it was there, along with some of the most delicious fish I had ever eaten and of course their own home cured prosciutto ham.

There was red and white wine along with rose and with champagne. The Mariachis played all evening and when it was finally over at approximately 11:00 p.m., I was completely exhausted and so went to my room which had one of lumpiest beds I had ever had the opportunity to have laid in, but at 11:00 p.m. and with so much food and wine inside of me, I didn't much care.

As I started to fall asleep, I had thought about the four days Juan and I had spent in the car as we traveled from the UK through France and all the way through Spain, and all the greasy burgers and french fries as well as all the Cokes and 7up's we had consumed along the way. His family had certainly made up for all of these insults we had forced on our stomachs in order for us to reach our destination in record time! I also imagined that I could possibly pick his mother-in-law's brain on how she had managed to cook such delicious seafood and would hopefully be able to reproduce them on future menus, or even food festivals. "Yes," I said to myself, "This could have been one of your better moves, Master Burrows, this Spain trip could pay off with big dividends . . . or would it?"

When I woke the next morning, I could smell something cooking in the kitchen, something delicious. I got out of bed and hit my head on a leg of pork that had hung above me. This was obviously how they had air dried the prosciutto ham. I got myself showered and ventured into the kitchen. Then Juan came into the kitchen with a smile from ear to ear which can only have meant one thing—that his reunion with his wife had been an enjoyable one. "*Buenos dias*, Señor Tony, *comos esta usted?*"

"Pardon?" was my reply. He said, "Good morning, Mr. Tony, how are you? We are in Spain now and you have to *hablo Español.*" And with that, he went over to his wife, who was cooking up a storm for our breakfasts, tapped her on the bum and said, "Ma chica bonita," and kissed her on the neck. *Good lord love us,* I thought to myself, *and to think he had driven for four days and nights to be with his wife.*

Love most certainly did work in mysterious ways.

We ate the frittata for breakfast and then Juan had offered me a tour of the village. You have no idea how happy I was that his wife was not going to be a part of the escort. It was going to take me a couple of days to get over the shock of that.

We walked along the seafront for about an hour or so and then into the village itself. It was then that Juan said to me, "My wife is very beautiful, Señor Tony, no?"

"*Si*, Señor—very." If he loved her, and she him, who was I to contest his choice of females.

As we walked through the village I saw a little lad of about five years old, playing with a stick and a hoop. All he was wearing was a dirty old T-shirt and that was it, no underwear, no socks, or shoes. Juan had said that he was from the poorest family in the village; I went up to him to give him a ten peseta note and he said to me, "*Muchas gracias*, Señor, *no me gusto.*" Juan informed me that his family were very proud people and had taught their son never to accept money from strangers. His father had had a job on a fishing boat but the owner had died leaving him unemployed. *What a shame,* I had told myself, *but how did he manage to keep his family in food and housing? God only knew!*

As we arrived back for dinner, Margareta sat on the porch way with a stunning young lady. She stood and was at least five feet five inches tall, had long black hair, huge boobs, a tiny little waist, and a bum to match. Margareta did the introduction. "Señor Tony, this is Angelica, Angelica, this is Señor Tony." Her smile melted my heart immediately. She was an absolute beauty and being a boob man, thought that she was perfectly proportioned.

We all sat and drank red wine mixed with soda water. This way you could pretty much drink as much of the stuff without getting wasted, until the early hours into the evening.

Margareta kept looking at me as if to ask for my approval. I was happy with her choice and could see that this month was going to be a great one; I gave her the nod—a wink of approval. We had agreed that the next evening we would go for a nice walk along the water front.

It was a romantic evening and I was looking forward to getting a bit of action as it had been at least six months since Jackie and I had broken up. Her parents had barred me from their house as I was round there so often while they weren't; they were worried that the neighbors had viewed their house as one that had become a knocking shop. As if!

Angelica showed up at the house looking more beautiful than ever but with a bloke! I looked at Juan as if to say, "What she has a boyfriend already?" Juan immediately said to me, "No, no, silly. It's her brother."

"So what the hell is her brother doing here?"

Then the penny (or peseta) finally hit the ground. He was her chaperone. "And," I said to Juan, "how often does her brother have to hang around like a bad smell?"

"Only until you propose to her," he said with that typical "Manuel" smile on his face. "So I don't think for one minute that if I were to propose that he get lost while I make mad passionate love to his sister in the sand dunes is going to cut it, right?" I hated Juan and his stupid "Manuel" smile when he said, "No, Señor." I was happy he was married to the wicked wench of the South because they most certainly deserved each other.

We walked along the promenade and then we said our good-byes. I shook Angelica's hand and then her brother's and as far as I was concerned that was it. But it was not it because the next day Angelica came around at approximately 10:00 a.m. screaming and shouting, "*Bastardo, bastardo!*"

On inquiring who and for what reason these profanities were aimed at, he said, in a very sincere manner, "You, amigo . . . you."

But why, I didn't even touch her last night!

So here was the issue. Juan had relayed my disappointment at having to share the evening with her brother last night and what I would have rather have done with her in the sand to his wife who had then told Angelica, who, now get this, was the half-sister to Margareta through a previous marriage.

Lord, give me strength! It was no wonder that Juan had married that woman. I bet the poor sod had no choice.

Needless to say, I was somewhat disappointed in how things were progressing and had decided to keep my distance from any of Margareta's potential "suitors."

The month slipped by with no other female companions from Juan's family in any event, not saying I didn't find any female company under my own steam, it just made it awkward when it came to bringing them home to "Mum" so to speak.

Speaking of whom, Juan's mother-in-law was I soon found out to be a stupendous cook and would love it when I would sit by her side, jotting down all the details as she would busily prepare our meals; in fact, it was Juan who had admitted in the end that his mother-in-law had become inspired by my enthusiasm that she had apparently pulled out the stops and so was producing a culinary extravaganza that was impressing everybody.

I think the best day I had had in that particular month was when we had heard that Jean Carlos's family, you may remember him as the little five-year-old who had nothing to wear but a dirty old T-shirt, well, in any event, his father had placed a ten peseta bet on the local lottery and had one a million pesetas. I, for one was overjoyed at the prospect of this polite, unassuming little lad, finally being able to wear some clothes that would at least cover his behind. His father had bought his own fishing boat and was making a small fortune fishing in the parts he had remembered as being some of the richest, whilst fishing with his friend.

One day, I had taken my young lady across to Tunis in Tunisia, which was a two-hour boat trip from Algeciras across the mouth that opened up from the Atlantic Ocean to the Mediterranean Sea and was astonished at the divide within the two cultures. Not realizing that Tunisia was a Muslim country, I was amazed at the fact that most women had their heads, mouths, and noses covered in a black veil, and the men wore robes that touched the ground.

Due to some strange looks at my bronzed, scantily dressed, beauty, we had decided to go into the first store we could find and bought her a pair of jeans as well as full length cardigan as the "cut-offs" and the tight-fitting T-shirt were causing too much of a stare.

It was a sad farewell at the Torremolinos Airport, firstly because I was saying good-bye to my Spanish girlfriend, Francesca, and then my friend Juan, who had been my lifesaver whilst working at the "not-so-sane place" at the restaurant, my co-driver from the UK through to Spain, and who had taught me to converse in Spanish. Both the in-laws were there to bid me farewell; Margareta had decided to stay home, which was no skin off my teeth, and yet, as much as I would have loved to stay, had decided that I had better get back to the real world, complete with my new recipes.

CHAPTER THIRTEEN

It's Off to Good Old Blighty

SO ON ARRIVING BACK IN England, picked up a copy of the *Caterer and Hotelkeeper* and started to look for a job, one of which was a second (assistant) chef in a place called Litchfield, and what seemed to be a nice little restaurant called Thrale's. It was an old abattoir and a butcher's shop as well as an old bakery that had been very cleverly converted into a bar (the abattoir portion) and a restaurant (the butcher's and bakery side of things) that had approximately sixty-eight seats.

I fell in love with this restaurant just as soon as I had walked into the kitchen to meet the chef by the name of Robert. A strange guy who had ginger hair and a goatee. He, I soon found out, was married to Lynn, one of the lunchtime servers and who, it seemed, was a bit of a nymphomaniac. I accepted the job and would start in a week's time and was informed that I could stay with one of the owners, of which there were three, until I had found suitable accommodation. This particular lady was a horseback rider and would go horse riding as often as she could, according to Lynn as this was when she would get her "jollies" (something to do with the positioning of the saddle to her crotch).

In any event, I had been there a week and had started dating such a pretty young lady by the name of Louise. She was, in my opinion, knock-dead gorgeous and worked as a server during the evening.

I was getting pressured by the horse rider to move out and so had found a bedsit that was approximately a five-minute drive from work and it was ideal.

The owner of the house was a lady by the name of Mrs. Ladner who I found to be such a gracious individual. She had an additional tenant who was a teacher (and a lousy one at that because he used to work at an elementary school and had been fired as a result of the low grades his students were achieving). I have just remembered that the day Mrs. Ladner had handed him his notice for the lack of his commitment as it had applied to his rent, so he went and opened all of the hot taps within the communal bathroom we had shared, and then blamed me for it! I remember it well because it was my birthday, June 27, and Mrs. Ladner had come to my room the same day to give me notice and had seen the two birthday cards I had received—one from Louise and the other from the chef's wife Lynn (?)—and had gone out to buy me a card, with an apology stating that the loser of a teacher had owned up to the fact that it was he who had *mistakenly* left the sink taps open.

In any event, I for one, was happy when he left as he had almost cost me my living arrangement to come to a close, which I was not happy with as I was very content living there.

Louise and my relationship had almost flourished toward the physical plane, but she had wanted to wait until she was eighteen (at this particular time she was seventeen and I was twenty-one so I respected her wishes). We did a lot together and I had become fairly close to her Mum and Dad as well as her older sister who was, I think, approximately four years older than myself and was already married. Her Dad was an ex-army man but had been stricken with bowel cancer and had undergone quite a few operations that had left him with a whole bunch of tubes hanging out from all over the place. I felt quite sorry for him as he obviously was in a bad shape and goodness knows how long he had left to live.

I can remember my first and only ever trip to Blackpool was with Louise and I recall sharing a bed with her, but as I had said, nothing ever happened which is why I probably got fed up with her in the end. When I think about it now, I had only three months to go before she was going to give herself to me but with the hormones of a twenty-one-year-old raging through my body, I felt that three months was going to be a lifetime and so had decided to move on, which made it particularly difficult for us at work as with me being on the culinary side of things, and she being on the service side of things; it just didn't work that well and so she left the restaurant.

Enter Lynn—the chef's wife. My goodness, she was hot (at least it appeared so to a twenty-one-year-old). When she used to work the lunch shifts and I used to have to go to the washroom, she would follow me and wait for me to come out when I had finished and would get me into a dark corner and start rubbing herself up against me and whisper rude things into my ear whilst sticking her tongue into it as well. She used to joke, quite openly, that I used to go round their house each Thursday for sex lessons. Chef would always ask me on Friday morning, "So how was your day off then, did you go anywhere nice?" And would give me a smile and a wink of the eye, almost as if he was trying to advocate the fact that I should give it a try. I knew for a fact that he would have no objections if it had in the end transpired with his wife for the following reason.

One day, Lynn and the chef had invited us all to a Christmas party at their home and Lynn was trying to hook me up with her friend who she assured me would be very "accommodating" when she wanted to be with me. Upon deciding that she wasn't my type, I got whisked into the bedroom by Lynn for what I thought was going to be a chat on "what the hell is wrong with you?" to what turned out to be a raging kissing session on the bed whilst I still had a beer in my hand and her hand down the front of my trousers.

At that particular point, who should walk in on us but no other than the chef, who simply said, "Oops, sorry," and walked straight out again. At this stage of the game, I had decided that I was getting myself in too deep and had concluded that enough was enough, and besides, she was thirty-eight years old and was ruining my reputation with the younger, prettier girls at work. The next day the chef smiled at me and said, "You know, I met Lynn in bed at a party!"

After the New Year was up, I had started dating a young lady by the name of Franky, who was as pretty as Louise, and was not working at the restaurant, but her mum was as a preparation lady. Sadly she fell into the same category as Louise, which meant that she (nor I) was not having any of my advances and so she was gone within a month.

Then came Valli (I know what you are thinking, "Really, Tony, two girls, in succession that together formed the name of a singer," but it was true). She was a lovely lady also, who lived in Brighton, nineteen years of age with the biggest set of boobs ever, so much so, I can remember my Mum saying, "She's a big girl, Son." To which I had replied, "Really, Mum?"

I soon realized my infatuation with boobs was just a passing phase, as the girls I had dated after Valli were much smaller in proportion and it was at this stage that I had realized that big boobs weren't the only asset I should be looking for in a lady.

After leaving Thrale's, I had decided to get a real job and so applied for a chef de partie position at the Hyde Park Hotel in London. Well, what an experience this turned out to be!

CHAPTER FOURTEEN

London Here We Come

I HAD ARRIVED AT THE Hyde Park Hotel with some great expectations, after all, this was one of London's finest that was a member of THF Group of Hotel (Or Truste House Forte). This was a company that used to be owned by the famed Italian hotelier Sir Charles Forte.

He had moved from Italy to Weston-super-Mare, where his father ran a café with two cousins. Charles's main training at the age of 21 came in Brighton, where he managed the Venetian Lounge for a cousin.

At 26, he set up his first "milk bar" in 1935, the Strand Milk Bar Ltd, in Regent Street, London, having thoroughly researched the location. Soon he began expanding into catering and hotel businesses. At the outbreak of World War II, Forte was interned in the Isle of Man due to his Italian nationality, but he was released after only three months. After the war, his company became Forte Holdings Ltd, and bought the Café Royal in 1954. In the 1950s he also opened the first catering facility at Heathrow Airport and the first full British motorway service station for cars at Newport Pagnell, Buckinghamshire on the M1 motorway in 1959. Sir Charles Forte was knighted by the Queen in 1970 and awarded a life peerage in 1982 as Baron Forte, of Ripley in the County of Surrey. He was also a knight of the Sovereign Military Order of Malta.

Trust Houses Group Ltd and Forte Holdings were merged in 1970 to become Trust House Forte or THF. Through mergers and expansion, Forte expanded the Forte Group into a multi-billion pound business. His empire included the Little Chef and Happy Eater roadside restaurants, Crest, Forte Grand, Travelodge and Posthouse hotels, as well as the wine merchant Grierson-Blumenthal and a majority (although non-controlling) stake in the Savoy Hotel.

The Grierson-Blumenthal stake was a "forced" acquisition by the group; it had originally been a personal holding of Charles Forte and fellow directors of the group, supplying liquor to Forte restaurants and hotels at substantial personal profit until concern in the late 1970s about prosecution under the Companies Act obliged the directors to incorporate Grierson-Blumenthal as a subsidiary.

Forte was the CEO from 1971 and Chairman from 1982 (when his son Sir Rocco Forte took over as CEO) of the Forte Group. Happy Eater and the five Welcome Break service areas were bought from Hanson Trust PLC on 1 August 1986. In the 1990s, the company was renamed as Forte Group plc.

Lord Forte passed full control to Rocco in 1993, but soon the Forte Group was faced with a hostile takeover bid from Granada. Ultimately, Granada succeeded with a £3.9 billion tender offer in January 1996, which left the family with about £350 million in cash.

Lord Forte died in his sleep on 28th February 2007 at his home in London, aged 98.

I had had the privilege of cooking for, as well as meeting Sir Charles on a number of occasions and he had always considered the Hyde Park Hotel one of his favorites.

This hotel had what I would call today a "full brigade."

There was the executive chef by the name of John Insley, a head chef by the name of Bob Worthing as well as four sous chefs, Magson (or Maggot as we used to refer to him), Jimmy Brosnan (a huge Irish fellow), Colin (the salt and pepper shaker), and Jason (the alcoholic). In fact they were all alcoholics apart from Bob, whom I had a tremendous respect for as a result. The executive chef (or John Boy) used to leave his office, on his way home, in his very fashionable dark blue trench coat and his pinstriped suit (he used to get changed in his office behind closed doors that would take him the best part of half an hour, enough time, we all assumed, to polish off the half bottle of Vodka that was delivered on a daily basis to the office, for cooking purposes) in order to leave by the side entrance, and after saying to me, "Goodnight, Tiny" I used to watch him literally bounce off the corridor walls as he would negotiate his way to the exit. He constantly stank of vodka and as chef saucier, I knew that we had not one dish that required vodka as an ingredient for the purpose of cooking.

Then there was Colin on the "salt and pepper shaker" on Mr. Condiment, as he couldn't make a consistent decision if his life depended on it (salt and pepper) and he used to shake continuously and perspired neat whiskey (or so it seemed) during service.

Then there was Maggot, so named because he has his head so far up John Boy's ass he should have been a Maggot. Nobody had any respect for him at all as he was a Yorkshire man, fat with thin black greasy hair, who when calling out the orders, would insist on using his own stupid accent, thus confusing the foreign chefs that we had in the kitchen. Half the time he didn't receive what he had ordered as a result. He got fired just before we left because most people would purposely screw up his order just to get back at him, and so he would have no control over the service.

Then there was Jimmy Brosnan or "Irish," as we used to call him. Each day, John Boy would order the kitchen boys seventy-two beers that would be delivered to the chef's office that was, coincidentally, right next to the sauce (my) section. As they would arrive, myself and Brian Hewitt used to grab approximately six to ten each and lock them in our knife drawer. This was more than our fair share, but I had figured that given the fact we worked in the hottest part of the kitchen we deserved to be reasonably hydrated, and besides this, they were a great bargaining tool should you need anything from the butcher's shop when it came to dinner time.

One particular day, I had gone on my break and had forgotten to lock my drawer and according to Rozaki, our Moroccan chef entremetier (or vegetable Chef), Irish, the large sous chef had helped himself to my beers, leaving me with just one.

With this in mind I had gone to the beverage store to get an empty Heineken bottle with a lid to match and had filled it with washing up liquid and vinegar, placed the cap firmly on top of the bottle and then had placed it in my "reach in" fridge to chill overnight. The next day "Irish" came into the kitchen and made a beeline for my reach in fridge, grabbed the bottle of suds, flicked off the lid, and shouted, "Just what the bleeding doctor ordered," and proceeded to drink the contents, without even taking a breath. Have you ever seen a guy throwing up vinegar and having bubbles belching from his mouth and nose? Well I have and I must admit it is bloody hilarious, particularly when it is a huge, beer-thieving Irish guy that is going blood red in the face and is continuously heaving up copious amounts of bubbles.

It was a sight to behold and despite Irish knowing who it was that had put it there, it was never mentioned it again. My beer stash was once again safe.

Now coming to *la piece de la resistance* as it relates to sous chefs, whose name was Jason. We called him Ginger. This guy was a strong and short ginger-haired git (hence the name) and was the biggest alcoholic of the lot. He could be a mean bastard also so when, for example, he would ask you to go into the chef's office to get him a sauce boat full of cooking brandy, you had better oblige or else he would turn your oven up while you had a pot full of demi-glace in the oven overnight cooking so slowly and find the next morning a pot full of black mush that was absolutely good for nothing.

Sometimes he would be so drunk that he used to hang off a roll of aluminum foil that was strung across the hotplate and we used to have to help him up off the floor and "hang him" back onto the aluminum foil. In fact, it was more than once that after hanging him back onto the foil a number of times that we actually left him on the floor and I would take over the control of service which was an absolute no-no in the hotel kitchen.

Once I remember leaving the hotel at about 9:30 p.m., and we were all going to our local watering hole by the name "Tattersall's." In any event, Ginger was on his racer bike and he was so drunk that whilst waiting at the set of traffic lights, had propped himself up against a car and was trying to figure out where the pedals were on his bike when lights had turned green and the car he had inadvertently propped himself up against, had starting pulling away. What I saw next had brought me to hysterics just writing about it.

It was dark and raining, and there was this drunk, sliding along the side of this car as it pulled off, while the drunk was still trying to coordinate his feet with pedals on his bike to finally run out of the car and then to fall off his bike, *then* to get up and start screaming at the car driver abusive obscenities for having driven off in the first place.

This was all over the kitchen by the time he had come to work. The next morning and on my way to work that day I had managed to purchase six bicycle bells that I had strategically positioned around the kitchen but out of sight so that every time Ginger had walked passed one of them, a cook could reach to wherever it had been placed and ring it. It was hilarious as we knew exactly where he was in the kitchen at any given time based on the ringing sound. What was even funnier was that because he was so drunk, he couldn't remember what had happened the night before and said to me, "Hey, Tiny, I keep hearing bells ring, do you?" To which I would reply, "No, Ginger, I can't hear a bloody thing, maybe you should go to see the doctor about that Ging because it could get quite serious, you know." And he did, on several occasions! I would organize days when we wouldn't use the bells at all, sometimes it would be a week or so and then a day, where if anybody so much as farted the bells would ring. We kept this up for weeks until John Boy got fed up with them and ordered them all removed. Git.

Ginger was the most skilled and could practically recite any garnish from *Le Repertoire de la Cuisine*. He could also be the funniest when he was sober. I remember an apprentice starting once and the first task he gave him was to chop a pound of flour for a full day and then on inspection the next day, threw it away and told him it wasn't fine enough and to start all over again!

We had an additional character by the name of Yogi Bear (this is what John Boy had christened him when he started at the age of thirty). He was now thirty-eight and was slightly mentally challenged. In the UK, it was law that the hospitality industry was obliged to hire people like Bear, who was our fulltime pot washer and sad to say, was the brunt of many a practical joke.

Bear loved his TV and would say to me sometimes, "Hey, Tiny did you watch *Bonanza* last night, it was on BBC one at ten." I had known that it was his favorite show and would purposely try to upset him by saying, "Nah, you don't still watch that crap do you? It's for poofters to watch." To which he would reply very angrily, "Well it's better than that crap you watch, what do you call it, *Tomorrow's World*?" Then I would calm him down by singing a few of his favorite such as "I'm All Shook Upy" or R. Whites's "Lemonadey" or say his favorite expression that was "Hey, Bear, do you fancy a bit of Rapesupy?" He was fat, ugly, and smelly and had sores on his head that he would constantly pick at.

I will never forget the day my friend and roommate Tim was working the fish section and Bear had walked passed him and had stuffed a bread roll into his pocket. Tim said to Bear, "Hey, I saw that you thieving bastard and if you don't put it back right this minute, I am going to call Granada and have them take away your TV—you fat, ugly, thieving bastard you!"

Tim was running for his life and Yogi was in hot pursuit with a knife in his hand screaming at the top of his voice, "I'm gonna kill you, you son of a bitch!" Poor Yogi!

On the accommodation stand front, things were pretty good. We lived in a place owned by the hotel by the name of Sinclair Mansions and mansions they were not, but having said this, they were adequate. My roommate, Tim, was the fastidious type when it came to cleanliness as well as tidiness, which suited me down to the ground. We had an arrangement that should he be bringing back someone for the night, on a moment's notice, I would move into the lounge and likewise, he followed the same rule.

On the odd occasion, I would have friends come down from Litchfield to stay with me in my abode, which meant Tim would graciously commit to the agreement and vacate to the lounge with his now steady girlfriend. This particular weekend I had two lady friends as well as a male friend by the name of Peter Duckworth. An unfortunate looking chap by all accounts, but a friend indeed. I also had a girlfriend that had been arranged by Brian Hewitt's then fiancée, Nicola, who was staying with me this weekend that made it a bit awkward.

I can remember my girlfriend by the name of Janet, getting out of my bed with her bra and panties on, bending over as she attempted to squeeze into her tight jeans, and Peter being fixated on her healthy bosom. I can remember thinking to myself, *Get a good look, buddy, because this is all you're going to get this weekend.*

It was Christmas Eve of 1979 and as a result of us all working and due to the lack of transport available on Christmas Day, John Boy had been able to convince the GM that in order for us to be able to work Christmas Day, it would be a good idea if we stayed in the hotel just for the one night. *Wrong!* .

We had all been to a local pub behind Harvey Nichols, which was just opposite the Hyde Park Hotel, and was a posh part of London. There was myself, my girlfriend, Brian and Nicola, Tony Shearer and Scotty as well as "Mouth" and "Chicken" who had rolled out of the pub a tad the worst for wear.

Tony Shearer was a strange sort of chap who lived in Sinclair Mansions along with Nicola and Brian (they lived below us) as well as a few others from the hotel. He lived in a bedroom of his own and had decided to rebuild his motorbike in his room so the reek of engine oil that was soaked in his bedroom carpet was a constant annoyance, as the smell would greet you as soon as you walked into the apartment. He was a confirmed alcoholic at the ripe young age of twenty, smoked like a chimney, and coughed like an old man. When it came to his ability to be able to consume copious amounts of alcohol, this Christmas Eve was no exception. As we had left the pub, Tony Shearer had decided that he wanted to jump onto the roof of a Rolls Royce, but in his drunken stupor, had failed to notice that it was a soft top and so went right through the roof that produced a terrible ripping sound. Little had we known at the time that he owner of the Rolls Royce was in the pub that the car was parked outside of, and to add insult to injury, a friend of the owner had just left the pub and had witnessed the whole affair.

To cut a long story short, the entire occupants of the pub had spilled into the street and were after us. I can remember a guy grabbing me and pushing me up against the railing shouting, "It's okay, I've got the little guy." when the guy who had witnessed the whole episode shouted, "No, not that one, the one with the black hair." At which point the guy let go of me and then started running after Tony Shearer. It took him all of five seconds to catch up with him and then I heard a sickening smack as this guy's fist made contact with Shearer's face and down he went.

When he got up, his eye was all bloodshot so Mouth and Chicken rushed him to the hotel and we started sauntering back and was just about to cross the road outside Harvey Nichols when a police car pulled up and two police officers got out of the car and pushed us up against the display window and said, "Did you guys have anything to do with the car top that was ripped?"

I automatically denied having even been within the area then Scotty started getting obnoxious with the officer and got himself arrested for being belligerent and I just kept my mouth shut.

Back at the hotel, Shearer was sitting on the toilet with a cloth covering his face; he removed it to show me what was promising a beaut of a black eye in the making. His eye had actually closed up already.

That night, despite having separate rooms, my girlfriend and I decided to sleep in my room only to have the duty manager burst into my room only to find the two of us fast asleep. He got fired as a result which was John Boy's way of giving management a swift kick in the "Niagara's" (Niagara Falls or balls).

The next morning, I felt it was only fair to let John Boy know that we had been in a spot of trouble the night before, when Shearer walked into the kitchen, sporting the most swollen blooded, black-and-blue eye I had ever seen. John Boy took one look at him and said, "What the heck happened to you?" Then I said to John Boy, "That's not all, Chef, last night my girlfriend and I were caught in bed together by the duty manager." His eyeballs rolled back as he said, "Bugger me, what next?"

As we sat down for our traditional Christmas lunch in the kitchen where the Chef would carve the roast turkey, Maggot, the Yorkshire sous chef was bringing some beer to the table and slipped dropping a six-pack onto "Mouth's" face causing him a nasty cut on the bridge of his nose that sent him to hospital to receive three stitches. John Boy just looked at me and smiled.

The following day I dropped knife on my hand and went to the hospital and received three stitches. All John Boy could say to me as he bandaging up my hand was, "Roll on bloody new year, Tiny."

The next thing we all knew was that we were being interviewed for Canada—that was Nicola and Brian, my girlfriend at the time, and myself. What an adventure? I could hardly wait.

CHAPTER FIFTEEN

Oh Canada, Our Home and Native Land

THE EXECUTIVE CHEF, DANTE ROTA, of the King Edward Hotel, Toronto, was in town and was looking some chef de parties as well as some pantry people, and rumor had it that we were ideal candidates, primarily because we were four from the same high-end hotel, so potentially, we were five percent of his brigade.

The notice had been posted outside the HR office and as soon as I had seen it, I went to see Brian and asked him if he fancied it as I knew this could be the chance of a lifetime.

I was best man at Brian's wedding and so we had become fairly close and I knew that if I wanted to venture off into the unknown, it would need to be with someone I could trust implicitly, and Brian was my man.

The King Edward Hotel was an old property that THF had taken over from the Sheraton group, who had definitely let the hotel drop in terms of the quality of product that it was potentially capable of becoming.

As with any renovation, there were delays to be expected and so, after having signed the paperwork with Chef Rota, we were all very keen to get moving. Our work permits would be ready for pick up at Toronto International Airport on our arrival in Canada, but due to construction delays, the actual start date for us had been delayed by six weeks.

Good old John Boy was having none of this and so had got on the phone to the HR director in Toronto and had said that if we weren't out of the hotel within the next week, we weren't going at all. The next day a fax came through giving us the flight details as well as the name of the person who was going to meet us at the airport, and so within a week, we would be on our way.

It was a tearful farewell as we were leaving the UK for at least a couple of years, I had told myself, but then what was two years when you looked at the entire life that we had ahead of us, and then we would be back in the UK in no time (thirty-two years later and I still do not live in the UK)?

It was a ten-hour flight on a British Airways aircraft that would take us to our new land of opportunity. We were all bundled up in our fur coats, expecting this "Great White North" to be almost like the Antarctic but upon arriving at Pearson International Airport, was quite surprised to find that it was actually plus twelve degrees Celsius.

We all bundled into the limo and sat there in our fur coats, sweating profusely, and headed off to the hotel we were staying at until we had found ourselves suitable accommodation.

Enter Craig Stoneman. A good-looking guy, who we had met at the airport and who had also been hired by Chef Rota and who hailed from Cheltenham. A very good friend of mine who to this day is still a good buddy of mine. I am looking forward to actually living the moment when he said to me, "Do you know what, Tony, one day we will be sitting on a porch somewhere, in our rocking chairs, with a piece of straw in our mouths, saying to each other in our hillbilly accents, 'Hey, son, do you remember when . . . ?' And we are going to laugh and cry as we reminisce the times that we had together, particularly the time as we were headed to work and as we had passed the loony bin and a young lady had decided to embark upon the street care with a huge pink balloon." Well to cut a long story short, the street car was packed solid and this young woman, along with her caregiver, had walked down the entire length of the vehicle completely oblivious of the havoc this balloon was causing, as it bounced from person to person. Well, there was not seat to be had until one young chap who was sitting next to Craig had decided to relinquish his seat to this female, who proceeded to sit next to Craig. The only trouble being that this huge balloon had managed to find its way between Craig and this woman and she couldn't quite understand why she couldn't sit on the seat fully so as to get comfortable and so was adamantly pushing this balloon against Craig, who in turn had been forced against the window. Well, we were in hysterics as Craig was trying to look cool about the whole thing but the more we laughed, the more the entire occupants of the street car became aware of his plight, and the more people were starting to laugh. It was hilarious and one that will no doubt, be on the agenda.

Hopefully this will happen if this *condition* I am in allows. In fact, I am going to make sure it happens, one way or another, no matter what!

I will get back to Craig a little later on in this chapter.

So on arriving at our hotel, we settled in within a moment and we all commented on how brown the grass was (that would be the grass that was not covered in snow). My partner had commented on how she didn't like the big city and the snow and how she wanted to go home, to which my response was, "Well you can do whatever you like but I am staying, after all, it is only going to be for a couple of years, right?"

We were treated to dinner that night in the hotel and felt very special. The assistant director of HR arranged for us to meet in the restaurant at 7:00 p.m. where she would be waiting with her husband (later to be christened "The Wanker" by all three of us lads) who was the manager of a private club and who proceeded to get plastered at the expense of the hotel. We had to carry him out to a taxi later that night so that he could get home. His wife was so embarrassed and was so apologetic the next day, we actually felt sorry for her.

In any event, they had a child, to which I am the godfather too and then got divorced approximately a year later.

We went to the hotel to meet the chef who, incidentally, had been fired the day of our arrival due to a fight with the GM, so instead we met up with the director of HR, who then proceeded to inform us that had she been hiring for the kitchen, she would never have hired "couples" as they could be problematic when it came to HR-related issues, something I couldn't comprehend at the time but would soon—well, four years later—figure out exactly what she meant!

There we were, no executive chef and an HR director who had made us as feel as welcome as a potential epidemic at a murderer's ward at a hospital for the criminally insane and—no leader!

Enter Rod, the chief steward, who would not be with us for much longer but who would walk around dragging his right leg behind him as he encountered the contours of the kitchen, constantly looking at his watch after ceremoniously having lifted his wrist above his head, as if he was shading his view from the sun, and would say, "Holy f——k, is that the time?"

Yes, he was one of the most unfortunate people who had been employed by whom? Nobody knew who or, if they did, were not going to own up to knowing anything about it.

Rod would be our leader and would assign us duties such as walking around the entire hotel looking for potentially homeless mops and brooms that he obviously had the propensity to account for as "I am the chief steward and they are my responsibility." It didn't take us long to appreciate the fact that Rod was so serious about his job that quite often I would suggest to him that on a specific day, I had noticed the alarming lack of mops and brooms, to which he would look at his watch again and shout, "Holy f——k, it's almost 2:00 p.m. and what time do you guys finish?" To which one of us would say in a panicked sort of way, "Shit, Rod, this only leaves us three hours to find this stuff, but we have to find them all before it is going home time."

Little did he know that Brian, Craig, and I had deliberately hidden them that same day, a few hours earlier, knowing full well that this would our "skive" tactic that would kill a number of hours within the next month or until such time as a new executive chef could be found who was qualified to lead this bunch of English rebels.

So whilst looking for these mops and brooms, approximately a week after our arrival, we had discovered, quite by accident, the eighteenth floor! This was an old "top floor ballroom."

This was the top floor of the hotel that had so much potential in terms of a food and beverage revenue-generating outlet as it had huge bay type windows with a massive kitchen that would seem to come alive with the hustle and bustle of chefs every time I walked into it.

Unfortunately, nothing was planned for this magnificent room so we had decided that while we had no leader, this could and would be our playground for the next little while. On searching for these so elusive mops and brooms, us three lads would normally end up on the eighteenth floor for a game of soccer or just to puff away on our newly favorite find—that being a packet of twenty-five Rothmans King Size that were half the price you would pay for in the UK.

One day I remember quite clearly that we lads had decided to avoid Rod for as long as we could, and had actually managed to avoid him for a whole two days. When he had caught us on the eighteenth floor on day three, he lifted his hand in the air to look at his watch only to say, "Well, where the heck have you guys been for the last two days?"

Craig went into fits of uncontrollable laughter, which is when I had finally realized that the game was up and this would be the last time we would be left out of Rod's sight forever. Well until he got fired, this was approximately a week later, for his obvious inability to control three chefs that had hailed from the UK.

Poor Rod. You know, I could go into so many more details as to the antics we used to get up to on our first days at the "King Eddy," and as funny as they would sound to Brian and Craig, I feel as if they could possibly bore you, so I will spare you the details.

A week after Rod had left we were advised that a new chef had been hired. His name was Jean Francoise Casari. A bit of a weasel-looking chap by all accounts, who was accompanied by a deaf executive sous chef (who shall remain nameless for the fear of potential lawsuits against the author, whereas, I am not concerned about the others that will be named in this book, until such time as I say otherwise, as they have all since died of AIDS).

In any event, I have to add at this stage of the book that the hotel industry was renowned for having its more than fair share of homosexuals (something to do with the unsociable hours, I guess), which incidentally, didn't bother me in the slightest as I was a man whose philosophy in life has always been and continues to be "live and let live." But the issue here is that we had not realized at this point of the game that the executive and his subsequent additional sous chefs were also "batting for the other side." So how can I put what happened next into context without sounding like a "noofter" myself. Well here goes nothing.

Whilst in the UK at the Hyde Park Hotel, Brian and I had adopted this terrible habit of when either one of us would bend over to pick up a dropped knife or a spare mushroom, we go up to one another, grab whoever it was that was bending at the time, and would proceed to imitate the "shagging" situation by grabbing hold of whoever had to be on the wrong end of this mock procedure, and well, pretending to do the biz. While this was all well and funny in the UK, we had neglected to consider that things in Toronto could be quite different, until that was when Brian was bending down to pick up a knife from his toolbox and I had seized the opportunity to simulate a good rodgering from the rear, only to have Jean Francois come around the corner of the sauce section to catch me in the act; and on top of it all, to have Brian howling like he was enjoying it all—well, what can I say?

It was the executive sous chef, who had been convinced by the executive chef that we be pulled aside and should be explained as to why the actions we had taken the day previously were totally inappropriate and that if we liked working in Canada, they should cease immediately.

I remember feeling a tad rebellious at the fact that I was being stripped of my freedom of speech but then realized that I was a guest in their country and so, should I decide to stay, then I had better conform.

Now Craig had a great sense of humor and I can remember one particular day when he was taunting a couple of workers who were working on the outside of the building, who could see us through the glass that surrounded the kitchen side of the sauce section. Craig called me over and said, "Look at these two morons." He had two fillet steaks on a platter and was showing them to the two workers and was saying, "So you would let the both of us shag both your wives for these two steaks would you?" They didn't have a clue as to what Craig was saying and so would nod like a couple of fake dogs that would sit in the rear window of a car, nodding at every movement the car would make, saying "yes."

The executive sous chef caught us doing this and so had the windows covered the next day with white plastic sealing tape that restricted our view out into the street. What a boring old fart this deaf French idiot was proving to be.

As the hotel team was getting larger (opening date, it seemed, was just around the corner), more and more key positions were being filled. There was this blond by the name of Christine Adler that caught everybody's attention. She had started her temporary position as uniform manager and I thought she would have been perfect for me but I had already brought my partner with me from the UK so felt bound to be honest.

Craig on the other hand had different plans, and why shouldn't he because he was, for all intense and purposes, a single guy.

We had found accommodation at a place called Parkdale, and had boldly gone to the assistant director HR with the news that we had in fact secured three apartments within the same unit. To say she was unimpressed by the look on her face, came a bit of a disappointment to us all, but it didn't take long for us to find out why. It was the city centre for drug use and distribution, and had the mental hospital that I have mentioned earlier on in this chapter, just about two kilometers from the location of our new abode.

So after approximately two weeks of living in this conveniently located apartment (it was on Queen and Ohare Avenue), I had happened to be waiting at the street car stop when all of a sudden, who should walk toward the same stop after having left our apartment building with wet hair but Christine Adler. My heart sank when she walked up to me and sheepishly said, "Good morning, Tony."

That bastard Craig had made his move and had wooed this blond bombshell with his rakish charm and good looks, and well to cut a long story short, it wasn't too long before Ms. Christine Adler had become Mrs. Christine Stoneman, wife of Mr. Craig Stoneman.

I remember the wedding very well as both Brian and I were the best men. Craig and Christine had decided to share a cottage on Rice Lake. This was at a place called Peterborough that could only have been approximately a ninety-minute drive from downtown Toronto.

We, as a group, had been there on several occasions prior to this. This particular night we had all had so much to drink that a few of us had decided to go skinny dipping.

Well, Christine's mum, a great lady by the name of Gertrude, was dating a war amputee by the name of Tom, who sadly was an alcoholic. Tom, having had a skinfull had come back from the lake's edge and had stumbled into the cabin, false leg and all, and had started to get a bit amorous with Gertrude who was having nothing of it as we were all sleeping in one very large lounge area and so it was most certainly not appropriate on Tom's part. I started to laugh as his wooden leg kept banging against the wooden frame of the bed. Gertrude was disgusted with his behavior and so moved to another side of the room, and so Tom fell asleep and started snoring in the loudest monotone that I had ever heard.

The next morning, I awoke to see Tom's wooden leg at the bottom of our bed, as if standing at the head of a grave of a buried, fallen hero. All it needed was a soldier's helmet perched on top of it, cocked at an angle, and it would have been worthy of a photograph.

We left the next day so that Craig and Christine could do what newlyweds would normally do, as we had a cooking contest that meant that we would be putting our culinary skills to the test to see if we were worthy of our positions (and what if we didn't make the grade, were we going to be sent back to the UK?).

What an absolute knobhead this guy was starting to become. I was starting to have my concerns about him because he kept asking where I was whilst we were in the kitchen. Was it because of the rumor that had gone around the kitchen that I was the ring leader when Rod had been fired and was responsible for the two-day disappearing act or because Dave Hammond, our newly appointed banquet chef, always managed to have obtained copious amounts of beer. I was starting to suspect it was the latter.

So the hotel opened (late as was usually the case) and after three months, I was promoted to junior sous chef. Jean Francois had decided to leave the kitchen world and start his own business, contracted AIDS and died approximately three years later along with Chowsky (who I hated as he was not only a noofter but as about as useless as a piece of wet noodle, and a spineless wimp on top of it all).

The new chef, Herve Martin, was my kind of guy—married, with kids, and a real chef. He barely spoke English and so I would speak to him in French, which for some reason impressed him so much so that when it came to moving on, it would stand me in good stead.

Unfortunately, he got transferred to Philadelphia, something to do with the new GM. Then we were introduced to chef number three. My God, what an ugly brute this guy was. Tall, fat with a red nose, and smelt constantly of alcohol. He was German and the biggest cowboy I had ever met. He was a "Food Cost" man that meant that he was not concerned about the quality of food that we were sending out, but more about his month-end results that were no doubt incentivized by a bonus scheme. He would go into the fridges and deep freezers and used to pick up old pieces of roast beef and say to me, "Pass it out. Come on, Burrows let's get moving and pass it out." I said, in all sincerity, "You mean to the staff cafeteria."

"No, no, you fool to the restaurant."

This was, in fact, the straw that broke the camel's back in terms of my respect for this culinary dipstick as from this peculiar, pug-faced excuse for an executive chef. On top of this, he was giving me a hard time for the staff cook who was screwing up the food big time. I said to him one day, "What do I get paid for, looking after some staff cook who doesn't know his ass form a hole in the ground, or our discerning guests?" This comment had him squirming and even managed a very weak, "Yes, you are probably right." And with this final admission of guilt, knew that I had the big fat, ugly, turd by the balls.

But you know the expression, "Vengeance is best served cold," and it was, and it was the best that I had ever!

It was probably a week earlier that Chef Martin had called Maurice and I into a bar, just around the corner from the King Eddy by the name of "Crab Tales." And he had a proposition for us both that being that he had been offered a job at The Pan Pacific Hotel in Vancouver and that the only way he could accept it would be if he had a full complimentary head team, that is, a potential executive sous chef that would start out as his fine dining sous chef and then a pastry chef (of which Maurice was the best I had ever seen in my full career).

So without further ado, I had convinced Brian, his wife, and my partner that we should give this German bastard a taste of his own medicine. (Brian was going to work at the Empress Hotel in Victoria along with David Hammonds and Craig Stoneman.) My partner went into his office first with her resignation letter; he picked it up, read it, and put it to one side and Brian's wife did the same thing, an hour and a half later. The stuck-up, arrogant SOB did exactly the same thing; then Brain went in with his, this time the old git could see a pattern forming and was becoming increasingly nervous so left the office. I then went in and put my resignation on his desk and waited for his return. He came back to his office, saw my resignation, and went a pale color. I saw him open the letter and he threw it onto his desk in a fit of rage and stuck his head of his office and shouted, "Tony!"

As it had happened, I had managed to time my arrival at his office to be able to come up from behind him and whisper, loud enough for him to hear, "Yes, Chef, what is it?" He started to swear at me and I cautioned him that this was no way to speak to a fellow management employee.

He then asked me to take a seat, offered me a beer, to which I graciously declined and he started to talk to me as if he was whimpering a tad. So I finally had him where I had wanted him for so long. After all the shit he had given me for not following the staff cook all over the place to watch his every move. Something a sous chef should never have been assigned and for all the times he had come to work, stinking of booze and in a chef's uniform that had been slept in and then ripping off my face for not having his coffee ready when I was monitoring the staff cook! Oh, how was I enjoying the way he was squirming?

He gathered himself together and managed to squeak out. "So why are you doing this to me, shouldn't we be sitting down, and discussing this?" I then said to him, "Like you and I would discuss the reason as to why you would give me constant shit for the stupid staff cook and all his mistakes and why you would treat me like your 'boy' just because your coffee wasn't ready when you would walk into the kitchen completely pissed from the night before." He had a look of disbelief on his face as if my holding to him to ransom was a sign of my contempt for him. Well, he was absolutely right as I had grown to despise this overgrown cowboy who had the audacity to call himself a chef.

"So where are you going to work, somewhere locally?" To which I replied, "What, and have you screw me over again once I have left here? No way! *We* are all going to work at The Pan Pacific Hotel in Vancouver!" This was like the sword that had finished off the dragon. He knew then that he had been outsmarted by us all as he knew the chef prior to him had been in Vancouver, but he had thought that he had been here for social visit and not with a huge shopping list of employees, for which he had been very successful, as he had also bagged a pastry chef as well as a fine dining sous chef, two very key positions when it came to opening up a five-star deluxe hotel.

It was a great day when we left the hotel, of course his lordship was not around to bid us farewell but then, who cared, not I "Gunga Din."

My partner was now six months pregnant. We had sold our condominium and were staying at a friend's house for two weeks before our adventurous journey across Canada. Maurice and Mary Milton had started their journey a couple of weeks prior to us as the chef had decided that he needed Maurice to try out some recipes.

I had planned a route that would take us up through Saut Sainte Marie, to Thunder Bay, on to Winnipeg to Medicine Hat (which is where I had promised to call my dad from), onto Banff, Salmon Arm, and finally Vancouver.

The journey took six days in total and with only a couple of minor incidences, one of which had us staying at the Holiday Inn in Winnipeg as a result of the car freezing to the ground and it not wanting to start for neither love nor money and the second one being that as we were travelling through Rogers Pass in the Rockies. One guy had called me crazy at even having attempted the journey on a practically bald set of radials, which I soon came to appreciate as when we had stopped at a gas station (or at least had tried to) due to the lack of tread on the tires, the car didn't stop and we just slid by. Luckily, there was a second one only a mile away, which I could see well ahead of the entrance and so I was like a pilot on his final approach, having plenty of time to control my speed and we finally filled up.

Never again!

CHAPTER SIXTEEN

We Had Arrived at Our New Home

O**N ARRIVING IN VANCOUVER, WE** had checked into the grottiest motel you could have set your eyes on. The cockroaches were by far the biggest I had ever seen and now, when I pass the motel on the way to the airport, a chill runs down my spine to think we could have slept in that shithole (it was for only one night) and could have possibly had these huge critters (they were two inches in length if they were an inch) walking on us, or our pillows, as we slept at night.

The Pan Pacific Hotel was magnificent as it stood on the pier with its "Five Sails" like feature that harbored the convention center, all white and majestic. I thought to myself, *Eat your heart out, you old German bastard,* when thinking about the King Eddy Hotel. Yes, this place was me, with the snow-capped mountains in the background and the ocean just a few feet away.

"This," I said, "this was what I could, and would, proudly call my new home."

After approximately a week we had moved into our new home at 276, East 17th Street, North Vancouver, which ironically, I drive past at least twice a week as I make my way to the office to drop off paperwork, as it is required for this particular job, but more about this later—much later.

I started work the following day, after having arrived in Vancouver, at our Water Street office. There were a total of three of us in this office from the culinary department, namely the executive chef, our pastry chef, Maurice and the fine dining sous chef, me—a far cry from the budgeted ninety-six that we were to open the hotel with. It was then, I think, that I had cottoned on to the magnitude of the job I had undertaken.

I was going to have to assist the executive chef in the opening of each and every kitchen, as well as assist in the hiring of the balance of the ninety-three chefs. Luckily, we had hired our banquet chef from the King Eddy just before our departure and so he should arrive within a month to assist in the opening of his kitchen.

Before departing from Toronto, I had created some pretty interesting dishes that I had intended to put on my menu in the Five Sails Restaurant and after approximately a week had been able to sit down with the chef to go over them with him. His response when looking over them was, "Tony, but these are incredible!" This was music to my ears as I had never opened a fine dining restaurant in my life before and I felt a boost of, "Yes, you can do this!"

The opening date had been set for January 9, 1985. My first child was scheduled to arrive January 5 and this was a big concern to the chef and myself as what would happen if he was late and arrived on the day of the opening, I mean, this was going to be the biggest day of my career and . . . ?

I sat with the chef and had gone over the "critical path" plans as it related to the hiring schedules, training plans, menu dry runs as well when each restaurant would open, the opening gala that was scheduled for January 9, etc. Luckily for me the Five Sails Restaurant was scheduled to be the last to open, so I had plenty of time to concentrate on the other areas of the kitchen; and on top of it all, both the chef and I were very comfortable with the preparation work I had done whilst in Toronto that we could put this particular portion of the project on the back burner—for now.

The most important people to hire when opening a kitchen are your management team. So we had a pastry chef, a fine dining sous chef, and a banquet sous chef, all we needed now was two sous chefs for the Café Pacifica as well as two junior sous chefs for the fine dining room and an executive sous chef. The chef had asked me if I wanted to take the job, but with all the work I had to do, already felt overwhelmed and so we decided to hire a temp from our sister property in Singapore.

Steve Halliday, who had been hired to open the hotel as general manager, was a huge inspiration to me (and continues to be so today). I had been in touch with head office in order to find us this assistant and so within approximately two weeks, we had our number two.

Along with the number two came a kitchen artist. These people, I would later find out, were an integral part of the kitchen brigade in Asia and would be responsible for some fantastic ice carvings as well as realistic, life-sized sculptures that would simply appear from a block of Styrofoam that would adorn a buffet.

We had started hiring our junior sous chefs at the same time as we had started hiring our "Rank and File" and I have to say were ticking along at a very expedient rate.

Now before we had hired the sous chefs, I had been given the dubious challenge of hiring a staff cook. Something I felt more than qualified given my previous experience with my last job. *Wrong* again, Mr. Burrows. I have to admit my hand was forced here as our assistant personnel manager had the perfect candidate and given the pressure I was under with everything that I had on my plate, buckled under the "need to find someone with reasonable haste." Well, I have to admit that when this "culinary wizard" came on board, I was suitably impressed for approximately ten minutes, or until he started on about his personal challenges that he was going through, by which time I had convinced the chef that this position was undoubtedly one that should, in the future, be handled by the HR department.

After approximately two more weeks, the management team was in place and we had hired seventy five percent of our culinary team. Things seemed to be looking good.

It was coming up to Christmas and we were going to enjoy our first Christmas off in years. We were back at work January 2 with only a week to go before the official opening was scheduled. Two days later, our little person had started to move around quite aggressively inside his mothers' belly. It was January 4 and we had decided to go out for a curry diner with some of our newfound friends. I can remember being awoken by my partner at approximately 2:00 a.m. on January 5 as she complained of severe stomach pains. I assured her it was probably the curry she had consumed with intense vigor the night before and turned over to go back to sleep, only to be woken again two hours later to be advised that her water had broken.

Lions Gate Hospital was only two blocks away from our house and so after a very short ride in the car, arrived at the emergency. (I can remember joking with her as to how much we could save on parking if we were to walk to the hospital but sadly, it fell on deaf ears.)

At 1:00 p.m., I became the proudest dad in the universe as I watched my 9 lbs. 6 oz. son being delivered into the world. I was somewhat concerned that he didn't cry straight away and watched with so much amazement as they took his little blue body to one side and hastily cleared his airways and then to see him turn form a deathly blue to a beautiful pink as he took his first breath after he had decided to cry.

It was indeed a miracle to see such an event unfold and then to have him, a moment later, in my arms wrapped in a soft blue towel. I looked down at him with a tear in my eye and whispered to him, "Welcome into the world, my little man. Your daddy is going to love you forever." And I still do today, more than at that moment when I held him for the first time.

I called my Mum and Dad and announced to them that Christopher James Burrows had arrived safely into the world and that he sent them both a big kiss!

The entire family was ecstatic and the flowers were coming fast and furiously from all corners of the UK.

I was the proud father of what Steve Halliday had said on seeing him a week later was "A beautiful child."

Unfortunately, the celebrations were short-lived as we had to be back at work the following day.

January 9 came upon us like a hurricane and it was to be all hands on deck. Chef had a fit, as when they were setting up the buffet (it was a Nautical theme), they had dropped one of the ice carvings as they were placing it on the buffet table. It was the king of the sea so the centerpiece to the entire display. The air was blue!

Two weeks later, we opened the Five Sails Restaurant to do magnificent accolades from some of the most discerning food critics.

We had done it!

Now the fun was to start. It was called botulism and almost killed three people.

After approximately six months, I had been promoted to executive sous chef and had managed to entice Brian, over from The Empress Hotel in Victoria, to take over my position as the fine dining sous chef.

Just before Brian's vacation to the UK, we had decided one Sunday to go to the rifle range out in Burnaby. We had taken Brian's white Ford Capri and were within approximately two hundred meters from the rifle range when Brian had decided to make a right as he thought he had missed the turning. He indicated to hang a right into a lay by when there was this awful *bang*. My seat back had broken, after having been twisted a good forty-five degrees off of central and Brian's had broken completely and was lying flat on his back with the car still rolling forward, at which point, I had managed to grab the hand brake to stop the car

We had been rear-ended by a two ton vegetable delivery truck.

The driver had got out to see if we were okay and at that point, we were fine, astonished that Brian's car was in the condition it was in and that we had pretty much come out of the collision unscathed and so started to exchange insurance details.

We had managed to right Brian's seat so that he could drive the vehicle home and my seat (the passenger's) was beyond repair.

After having completed a prescheduled barbeque, and after all our guests had left, had decided to lay on the couch with Chris (it was past his bedtime and he was letting me know that it was time for his bottle, so I complied with his wishes). After approximately twenty minutes and after a few familiar sounds that had come from his diaper (I think eruptions would be the best way to describe them), had decided that this little man deserved a change. As I tried to get up out of the couch, I had experienced this excruciating pain from my neck down to the bottom arc of my back and for some reason, could not move my neck.

It was in fact whiplash that had me in traction for the next six weeks (an hour at a time, six days a week) as well as an out of court settlement of $7,000! Now where did that money go? God only knows (but can hazard a guess).

Whilst Brian was away in England on vacation, his assistant, a French junior sous chef, had decided to pickle some wild mushrooms but had not sterilised the containers beforehand. So one fine day, we had a call from the health department claiming that seven people had been admitted to hospital with suspected botulism poisoning and they had all claimed that they had eaten the night before in the Five Sails Restaurant.

Enter Steve Halliday, who immediately called a press conference asking that should anybody else was not feeling well as a result of eating in the restaurant, they should seek medical advice immediately. This was considered a bold and brilliant move on Steve's part as it meant that he had come clean and so this gave the press nothing to report on.

As it happened, it was an oriental waiter who worked in the restaurant, who had eaten off the plate of a returned dish and it was the mushrooms that were deemed the culprit. The health inspectors came around and closed the restaurant and took all twelve remaining jars of mushrooms for analysis and it was confirmed that these mushrooms (chanterelles) were the culprit, but in order to play it safe, everything (and I mean everything) that was in the fridges as well as the deep freezers had to be thrown out. This included ten kilograms of goose liver, fifteen kilograms of glace de viande, all the seafood and meats that had been prepared for a total of in excess of $30,000. It broke my heart to have to have thrown all these expensive items away but we had no choice.

To cut a long story short, nobody died, although the oriental server was on a respirator for quite a while and Steve very smartly sent all the seven affected by this botulism a beautiful Christmas tree that had been professionally decorated, along with some magnificent hampers.

I will never forget Brian's comments as I broke the news to him on his return from vacation. They were too derogatory to put into print, suffice to say his respect for the sous chef involved had hit rock bottom and so had to work on the sanitizing of the entire kitchen until such time as we had been given the all clear to reopen the restaurant.

I had thought that both the chefs, as well as my culinary career, were over but Steve rose to the occasion once again and we all kept our jobs (even the offending sous chef)!

The next six months was designed to rebuild the reputation of the Five Sails Restaurant, which Brian had managed to do, then came the best part of working at The Pan Pacific Hotel and that was the entire company wanted us to work in their hotels and this meant transfers.

While waiting to see where we would be going, the second best thing that would ever happen to me was happening right before my very eyes, the birth of my beautiful daughter, Michelle Elaine Burrows. She was so cute but a heavy 9 lbs. 8oz. My dad had commented on where these big babies were coming from and we joked about whether or not the milkman was a big guy. Little did I know that this little angel was going to melt my heart each and every day while she would grow into the beautiful woman that she is today.

After approximately three months, we had heard that Brian was off to Vanuatu (South Pacific) as executive chef and I was off to Kuala Lumpur (Malaysia) as executive chef. I was the last to be transferred for quite a while as the hotel had lost approximately 50 percent of the kitchen management team and so it was thought that enough was enough.

We had all been to the doctors for our relative shots (I wanted to murder the doctor as he made both my kids cry when sticking the needles into their arms) but then thought to myself that it was probably my fault for having accepted the transfers in the first place.

CHAPTER SEVENTEEN

Southeast Asia (Part 1)

I CAN REMEMBER THE DISCUSSION I had had with the GM of The Pan Pacific KL as we toured our hotel in Vancouver during the GM's conference that we had hosted in Vancouver. What an event that was. We had most certainly pulled out all the stops for this monumental event that had showcased the entire Pan Pacific Company and I had seen, for the second time, something that only Steve Halliday could have pulled off.

With a magnificent culinary theme that took the entire Pan Pacific management team from the east coast of Canada, all the way to the west coast with their subsequent destination, that being Vancouver; I felt that we had put Vancouver on the map. As did Steve, as the accolades that followed showed his true appreciation for the tireless efforts that we had put in for the company.

As we toured the hotel, my potential new boss cautioned me on how Southeast Asia had the potential to ruin marriages. The temptations were "endless" he had advised me.

We boarded the Malaysian Airlines flight to KL, which would take us at least fourteen hours, from Vancouver. The kids were great and Michelle slept most of the way in a bassinette.

When we had arrived in KL, we entered the country on a visitor's visa and there to meet us was the executive chef that I would be taking over from. He and I grabbed our suitcases and shoved them into a waiting limo and we were off to our new home of two years.

At the hotel, we were ushered up to a suite where most of my new brigade would be waiting to welcome us. It was as we were sipping a glass of wine and enjoying some hors d'oeuvres that Michelle (who will be referred to from hereon in as Squibs), had decided to fill her diaper with the smelliest poo one could ever imagine possible and was crawling in between all the chefs when we noticed it was leaking out of her diaper.

How embarrassing was this? Very!

The next morning, I was up at the crack of dawn ready to take the world by storm. I was introduced to the Executive Committee (which, I was now a member for the first time in my life).

Here, I met the GM (once again) along with the director of finance, the director of food and beverage, the director of sales and marketing, the director of engineering, the director or public relations as well as the executive housekeeper and the resident manager. We were quite the mixed bag of jelly beans in terms of expatriates ranging from the top man being Australian, Japanese to Malaysian to German and French to now a Canadian/English executive chef.

Until today, I have never worked with such a dysfunctional team such as this. The resident manager was always bad-mouthing the GM and fighting with the director of F&B; the director of F&B hated him back with a vengeance and was always fighting back with the resident manager (or RM from now on); the executive housekeeper seemed always to be giving me a hard time (something to do with two world wars and a world cup too) and the GM just sat there, watching it all going on, oblivious of the fact that this dysfunctional family were so unhappy with each other. Had he taken the time to sort it all out, believe me, we could have been a dynamic team.

I can remember being hauled into the GM's office one morning, then being promptly being advised that my food cost was way too high and that the GM had sent a letter to the regional VP of operations (copied to me, naturally), stating that I had been informed of the fact and was in the process of "sorting it out." Now high food cost could mean one of many things, but predominantly either the food items on the menu were too low priced or that a whole bunch of food items were walking from the kitchens. I had suspected the latter of the two as we had just changed all the menus within the hotel and so was pretty confident that they had been professionally costed by myself and given the fact that one of my executive sous chefs had advised me that the butchers were both of Indian descent and as all Malaysians would say to me, "Do you know what, Chef, if you were to be walking in the jungle and you had a gun, and you had met up with a snake and an Indian, who would you shoot first?" To which I replied, "Well, the snake of course."

"No, chef," came back the answer. "The Indian because you can trust a snake, to a certain degree, but Indians?"

I was shocked at such a statement given that 25 percent of the Malaysian population were in fact of Indian descent, only to be forced to fire both of them the next day because those sneaky bastards had been putting whole tenderloins of beef as well as whole strip loins of the same that would be vacuum packed, therefore completely safe from contamination, into the bottom of the pig swill containers (that were seventy-five gallons deep) and have then removed by the pig farmers (which every hotel would do) only to have the pig farmers sell them off (probably back to our hotel) at a reduced rate, thus pocketing a small fortune.

How long had this been going on for? Possibly since my arrival there, as this was the second time in three years that they had been caught and the last time was six months prior to my arrival, when they had been given a warning—basically a slap on the wrist as it looked as if the previous chef had been "in" on the deal and so had protected them against any serious disciplinary action!

What a place Malaysia was, so mystical when compared to Vancouver. I can remember our first day out with the kids. We had been there for an approximate three weeks when I had finally given myself the day off. The first of my new sous chefs by the name of Ron Brooks had arrived from Palau in Micronesia. He was most certainly a welcomed addition to my team as he had this "worldly" air about him and would soon become a very good buddy of mine, along with Walter Wiess and an even better buddy of mine, Erik Rufer (whom I have kept in contact with as a result of Facebook as well as through regular e-mails and who has very kindly given me his most valuable input as it relates to the contents of this book). Erik was a tremendous help to me as I embarked on my first trip to Southeast Asia, and who would pop up again once we had landed in Indonesia. Sadly, Ron passed away December 9, 2009 of prostate cancer that has prompted me to go each year, to have a check-up.

In any event, we were out for the day with the kids and what a day it was too. We had decided to take Squibs in her stroller, which proved to be a big mistake as the sidewalks, it would appear, were in such disrepair that the small wheels of her Canadian-made stroller were constantly getting stuck in the cobbled sidewalk, which did not allow for a comfortable ride within the almost confines of the hotel, and had us turning back within ten minutes and then venture off in a taxi to a park so that the kids could run around freely.

I had been warned about the taxi drivers and the "antics" that they could (and would, at every opportunity) get away with. I had come to realize that as a newly arrived expat family that had literally just gotten "off the boat" that we were to become fair game to anybody that was willing to take us for a "ride."

Needless to say, and until today, I have no regard for these vultures who pull up beside you as you wait outside of the hotel in their crudely painted yellow and black rust buckets, who drive like they have nothing in the world to live for, in and out of traffic, as if their lives depended on getting you to your destination of choice within the quickest possible time, only to try and charge you double the metered amount because they have the AC on all the way. I tried had to explain that had I been given the choice, I would have chosen not to have had the AC on all the way, only to have this particular driver, lose command of all his English speaking skills when it came to negotiating the price. On throwing the money at him on exiting the taxi, I was promptly told to "fut you." I had decided that quite possibly, it would be a good idea to buy a car just as soon as it was possible.

Chris and Squibs hated the heat as well as the fact that everywhere they went people would touch their fair skin as well as their hair. Chris was in the Montessori school at the age of three and a half years. I can remember one day taking him in the car we had just purchased (a Proton Saga) when he had said to me, "Daddy, when I get to school I want to show you which one of the boys is my best friends." When we arrived at the school I said to him, "Which one, my little man?" To which he replied, "There you go, Daddy, the one with the black hair." Bless him, Chris was the only one there who had blond hair as the rest of the kids were all either Malaysian, Indonesian, or Japanese, and so all had black hair.

This Montessori school was excellent as it taught the children basic systems of cleanliness; for example, when they had finished eating their lunch, they would have to neatly stack their plates in the sink ready to be washed up with the knives and forks separate and then go and wash their hands and dry them properly, before they could continue with their next task.

Living in the hotel had its benefits also, apart from having no rent to pay, all the essential services were free—for example, rooms service, food in all the outlets, housekeeping, laundry, etc. We had the full use of the pool whenever we wanted which I thought was excellent as Chris was an accomplished swimmer by the time he was four years of age. I, on the other hand, became a fairly good squash player as we had four courts that were hardly ever used and so playing a good game of at least an hour, three times per week, had me in great shape. My cholesterol level was way over the top at the time and so this amount of strenuous exercise certainly assisted with bringing it in line.

On top of all this, we got paid in U.S. dollars which was great as the exchange rate for U.S. into Canadian was 1.5 times more, which meant that for each U.S. dollar we were paid, we would get $1.50 Canadian. Also, as an expat, we had to pay a small amount of our salary into a provident fund to which the company would also contribute, which meant at the end of our tenure, we would have a nice little nest egg to take back to Canada.

A super bonus was that should we want to go and stay at our sister property, The Pan Pacific Resort Pangkor (an approximate two and a half hour drive up to the west coast of Malaysia on Pangkor Island) and as an executive committee member, we could stay and at no charge for the accommodation and 50 percent discount on all food and beverage. At one point, they had fired the Japanese GM and had imported a Canadian colleague of mine from The Pan Pacific in Vancouver, which meant each time we went there, it was all free including a beautiful beachfront bungalow with all the food, beer, and wine we could consume. Needless to say, we were up there once a month, and enjoying ourselves immensely.

Also the hotel was very generous when it came to family members coming to stay with us from anywhere in the world, allowing us to entertain them in any of the restaurants within in the hotel, free of charge.

I will never forget the time when my dad came down to visit us and we were on our way down to breakfast with Squibs. I was dressed in my chef's whites (so it was pretty obvious which part of the hotel I was working in) as the elevator door opened, it was almost full to the brim but we were very kindly beckoned to enter. So there we were, a granddad, a dad who was dressed for a busy day within the culinary world, and a sweet, innocent—or so it seemed—little two-year-old, dressed as if butter wouldn't melt in her mouth, with her golden locks of hair so neatly brushed and parted complete with a pretty bow, when all of a sudden there was a rip rawing noise that had erupted from my daughter's backside. On squeezing her hand, I said to her. "Michelle, what do you say?" Expecting a "Pardon me, Daddy," only to have her look at my dad, with the biggest and proudest smile on her face and so nonchalantly explain to my dad, "Hey, Granddad, I've just farted."

Well, I was so embarrassed, I had no idea where to put my face. My dad had streams of tears running down his face with laughter and the entire elevator seemed shocked that such verbiage should explode from a two–year-old's mouth. Given that we lived on the twenty-seventh floor of the building, I can only express my discomfort at the long twenty-four floor journey I had to endure, until reaching the ground floor. Bless her aye!

It was a touch of the good life that was for sure!

As a fairly new team member to the Southeast Asian region, my culinary repertoire was increasing as well as my management skills. I had a head Japanese chef, along with a head Malay chef, as well as a head Chinese chef and two executive sous chefs, and a corrupt chief steward. This guy had actually gone to the Government to complain that I was anti-Muslim, simply because I had questioned his ability to actually keep a kitchen clean when, on a monthly inspection, we had moved a fridge that had been in the staff cafeteria for just over two years, only to have an entire cockroach mass exodus from the back of this particular fridge. It was disgusting and something I should never wish to see again. Luckily, we had manned ourselves with cans of cockroach-killing spray that allowed me to personally count a total of 1,700 of these critters, after we had pulled the fridge out and disturbed them. It was the director of HR who had saved my neck as a result of his statement that had undeniably refuted the claim of the chief steward.

Apart from this, I think one of the other benefits of being an expat was the ability of being able to afford to travel. Something I had always appreciated as Chris and Squibs had circumnavigated the world twice by the time we had come back to Canada. But having said this, I think our trips to Singapore as well as Penang to stay at the Rasa Sayang Hotel on three occasions were among the most memorable, not to mention our trip to Terengganu, which was a place just south of Thailand, on the northeast coast of Malaysia. Here we were treated to the actual laying of some seventy-five green leatherback turtle eggs by a mother who had come ashore at approximately 11:00 p.m., swiftly followed by at least a half dozen more, and had dug a hole that was a good four feet deep into the silky soft sand and had proceeded to push out all of these eggs out in an effort to keep her species alive. Her eyes were covered with what looked like a thick mucus, as she struggled so desperately hard to dig this hole and I felt the compassion to wipe it out of her eyes as the constant flicking of sand had joined this mucus, but naturally could not intervene in what I understood as a miracle unfolding before us. As Chris, Squibs, and I stood there on the beach, I can remember the tour guide picking up one of the eggs only seconds after it having been laid and being offered a touch of it. It was warm and of a leathery texture, one that both my little kiddies didn't either like or appreciate, but for me, being a National Geographic buff, was in absolute awe of.

The next morning, we went back to where this miracle had happened, to find that the eggs had been removed by conservation authorities and had been placed into an enclosure that was protected from any predators by being covered with a wire mesh with last night's date and time of arrival.

As we stood and watched what had been several of the enclosures that had been painstakingly prepared, one of them had started to erupt as these little tiny baby turtles that had obviously been buried some time earlier, began to surface. This time, as they all tended to scurry toward the edge of the enclosure that was closest to the water's edge, the conservationist picked them up and placed them into a bucket for the safe transportation to the waves that they had naturally been conditioned to head toward, at the same time, handing one each to Chris and Squibs to hold for a short while. I could tell that they were suitably impressed by these little creatures as we walked them down to the shoreline to release them into the wild. A flock of birds had gathered overhead waiting to swoop down on these little miracles only to be scared off (for now) with blasts from an air gun that shot out only blanks, but would scare these predators away long enough for these little miracles to get approximately twenty-five feet away for the edge of the shoreline and a decent chance of surviving the perils that would await them in order to be able to return to their birth place, in years to come.

It truly was a memorable experience that had the kids bombard me with a ton of questions, some of them easy to answer and some not, for example, "Daddy," came Chris's first of many, "why do those birdies want to eat our little friends?" And then Squibs asked, "Daddy, can we come back tomorrow and see them again?" I was assuming that they hadn't understood the concept that they had gone forever and we would never see them again. On explaining this to them both came to obvious one of "But why, Daddy?" to the floods of tears that followed. Bless them. Then I said that they had gone out to sea to find their Mummy who was waiting for them. This seemed to stem the flow of tears and then Chris came up with the clincher. "But, Daddy, how will this know which one is their mummy?" To which I replied, "The same way that your daddy knows who you are."

This seemed to quench their thirst for some information that I soon came to appreciate and, it would be unique to my kids as, after all, how many of the children they would be meeting back in Canada, could actually boast at having experienced such a marvel.

The answer was none!

After having been at The Pan Pacific KL for two years, the GM had asked me to extend my contract for an additional year and given there wasn't much going on within the company, had reluctantly, decided to go for it. There was a rumor that the director of food and beverage (Erik Rufer) was moving on and that I stood a very good chance of getting the job but politics prevailed and it was given to a local chap who, on the arrival of the new GM, had wished he hadn't taken the position and I, after hearing this new GM threaten the F&B guy to "have his blood all over the walls of his office walls if the new menus were not in place by a specific date," had decided that it was a good thing I hadn't taken the position after all.

This guy (who shall remain nameless) was, in my opinion, an absolute tyrant and had his favorites within the hotel (of which I was not one of them) and of which one of my executive sous chefs was, and who seemed to get great pleasure in showing me what this new GM had in store for us when asking him over a couple of beers; I had intimated that he was okay and yet when it came to me, all he did was suggest my days could be numbered by showing me the imaginary slit from ear to ear with a make-believe knife.

It was this that had prompted me to call Steve Halliday (who had, by now, risen to the ranks of regional director of operations and was now based in Singapore) to ask if there was anything else going on within the company that would suit me. I had briefed him on the situation within the hotel, as well as the discussion with my executive sous chef, and was advised to hold on for a bit longer. The very next day, I received a call from Steve advising that the GM of The Sari Pan Pacific in Jakarta (Chris Green) was looking for a director of food and beverage. Chris and I had worked previously at The Pan Pacific in Vancouver (he was the opening director of sales and marketing). In actual fact, Chris was the number one employee of The Pan Pacific Vancouver Hotel.

I thought about it and decided to go and see the GM and get some info on the property as he had been transferred from Jakarta before being posted to KL. I should have known that he would highly recommend that I take the position as he no longer wanted me in the hotel, and upon relaying the conversation I had had with my executive sous chef and the slitting of the throat scenario, he replied with a grin on his face. "Well, you didn't hear it from me." Which only confirmed to me that should I decline the position at the hotel in Jakarta, then I would no longer be employed within the company.

I called Chris Green the next day and accepted the position and asked when he would like me to start and reminded him that my third child was almost done and that we would need to fly back to Malaysia at some point in time as my child's delivery had been scheduled and booked into the Subang Medical Centre close by to the airport on or around the expected delivery date of August 12. Chris and Steve were fine with this and suggested that we fly down to Jakarta within a week and to check the place out, then as the delivery date grew closer, my partner and my third could fly back to Malaysia and would stay at the PPKL, and then I would fly back to Malaysia within a day or two and then we would all fly back, as a family, to Jakarta.

So the plans were in place and my second son was born on August 12 (after having been induced).

I called Mum and Dad and advised them that Daniel Jason Burrows had arrived safely and had weighed in at a whopping ten pounds! For some reason, when I held my boy in my arms, I had a feeling there would be more to this lad than would immediately be apparent. And I was right!

What was also a tad amusing to me was that after Daniel had been born, I had an exact week to get him his Canadian citizenship before I had decided to seek Malaysian citizenship for him, which I had been informed, would never be allowed by the Malaysian government. I afforded a smile and said to myself, "As if?"

CHAPTER EIGHTEEN

Enter the Big "C"

I HAD FOUND A LUMP on my partner's breast and so we had decided to go to the local cancer clinic. The examining doctor had suggested that we go to Singapore. I called Chris Green who had immediately got on the phone to Sempati Air and booked us two tickets to Singapore for the following day. At 3:00 p.m. and on checking the passports, we had discovered that our exit visas were no longer valid and so Chris, with the assistance of our Director of Sales and Marketing Ibu Hetty Soemartono, had called in all the favours from as many government officials as were available, and had managed to get a hold of someone who could assist us. Bless this lady as, without her kindness and influence, God only knows what sort of a mess we would have had to face!

At 7:00 a.m. the next morning, and on arriving at the airport, we were whisked through customs and both passports stamped with a multiple exit visa, signed in green (as were all government documents) and sat in the departure lounge waiting for the 9:00 a.m. flight.

Sempati Air was owned by one of the Soeharto brothers (the son of the president at the time) and was renowned for refreshingly departing on time, as opposed to the rest of the country operating on, what was casually referred to as, "Rubber Time." On top of this, they would hold a raffle whilst you were in flight and the person who sat in the lucky seat would win a complimentary flight on any one of their next flights to Singapore. Little did we know that for the next six months, we would become regulars but despite this, did not win a free flight.

On arriving at Changi Airport, we hailed a taxi and headed straight for the Mount Elizabeth Hospital that had an oncology department that was reputed to be one of the world's best.

We went to see the specialist that had been arranged by the doctor in Indonesia at 1:00 p.m., and we were assigned a bed by 4:00p.m. I was amazed at the speed with which this had all been arranged and had put it down to the ever efficient Singaporean style of operating, then had the sick thought that maybe this was as a result of our situation being more serious than we had been led to believe.

The operation was scheduled for 9:00 a.m. the next morning where a biopsy would be performed and if all went according to plan, she would be back in her bed for 9:30 a.m., if not, then it would be 11:30 a.m. before the anaesthetic would have worn off.

I left the hospital and went to my hotel room at The Pan Pacific Singapore and ordered room service and started to plan my options if all did not go well the next day. I had three children, the youngest of whom was only five months, how on earth was I going to tell them if the news was not good.

We had learned that the probable cause of this cancer was that she had decided to have a third child as she did not "feel complete" (there was no history of cancer within the family). I thought to myself, *What a huge price to pay so that you could just feel complete.*

The following day, I had arrived at the hospital at 6:00 a.m. having not being able to sleep a wink all night and what I had walked into was met with this hysterical woman who looked at me and cried, "I am going to be all right, aren't I?" To which I replied, "Of course you are!" What do you say to a woman who is just about to have a potentially life changing operation?

The surgeon came in to see us at 7:30 a.m. and said to me as we walked out of the room that he would be performing a biopsy, and that if he needed to go ahead with the surgery, he would let me know. At 8:30 a.m. she was prepped and at 8:50 a.m. she was anaesthetized and at 8:55 a.m. she was on her way.

I sat and waited in fear in the recovery room as the surgeon performed the biopsy then within ten minutes, he came out of the operating room, carefully preventing his hands from touching anything and being assisted by a nurse with the door, announcing that the tumour was in fact malignant and that he would need to continue with the operation.

I felt completely hopeless at this point and so decided I should call my parents who in turn, should call her parents advising them of the news.

It was, by far, one of the hardest calls I had ever made in my life.

She woke at 11:35 a.m. and the first thing she said to me was, "What time is it?" I said to her, "It's 11:35."

"I knew it," was all she said before falling into a medically induced sleep.

That particular weekend, the GM's of all The Pan Pacific Hotels had met up at The Pan Pacific Singapore Hotel for their annual conference and one of the topics on the agenda was health coverage. (Apparently we, as expats, were only covered for an insurable value of U.S. $10,000, and here was I in a hospital in Singapore with a cancer patient!) It would appear that the timing was spot on as in my case, I was the perfect example of what could happen to anybody who was living abroad and were at the mercy of the medical profession. My case was brought up at the conference whereupon Steve Halliday (who was now VP of operations) had deemed it fit that the company foot the entire bill for our stay in the hospital which, I had later found out, came to approximately U.S. $37,000!

After I had left the hospital room for what the nurse had told me would need to be for a good four hours, I went to the hospital admitting area and was contemplating my next move when Steve Halliday, along with Chris Green and the president of the entire company, walked through the entrance with a huge bouquet of flowers. Steve asked at the reception that they be delivered to the room and asked me how the operation went. All I could say was, "Not good, Steve, the lump was cancerous."

Steve gave me a hug and said to me, "Well, you are with family now and I don't want you to worry about a thing."

It was the next day that I was summoned to the Dr.'s office advising that, due to the aggressive nature of my partner's cancer, that I should seriously consider getting the "snip" as, if she were to fall pregnant again, it could have a catastrophic outcome, so I had agreed to it.

Boy what an experience this was too. It felt as if somebody had decided to get my testicles in a vice and then started pulling them from my entire body. In fact my eyes have started watering as I am relaying this portion of my book to you!

We left the hospital after only a few days and headed back to Jakarta where the children had been staying under the watchful eye of Yati, our maid, as well as every female that worked in the hotel, carefully monitored by my wonderful secretary by the name of Endah.

It was the next six months that proved the most challenging as despite the actual surgery that was performed was only a lumpectomy, and so the actual recovery was not that long, we had to fly to Singapore each month for chemotherapy and then required seven weeks of daily radiotherapy. Enter Steve Halliday and Chris Green *again* who had very kindly arranged for my entire family (excluding me of course) to stay at The Pan Pacific Johor Baru for the duration. This five diamond hotel was conveniently located at the border of Malaysia and Singapore and so made for an hour's bus ride to the hospital each day, so it was the perfect solution.

After my two years were up, my contract wouldn't be renewed as the family insurance for us had escalated tenfold and so we were no longer affordable for a hotel to pay for.

I was sitting in the Melati lounge one day and who should saunter up and sit down beside me but my dear friend Erik Rufer who, as you may remember, used to be my director of food and beverage at the Pan Pacific Kuala Lumpur. He had landed a GM job in Yogyakarta and so we were able to rekindle our friendship once again, and this meant playing a lot of golf at Halim Golf Course, something I enjoyed immensely. In fact Erik was one of the first people that we had met whilst living in Southeast Asia to come and visit us on our return to Vancouver, and who has helped me tremendously by proofreading my book. So a huge thanks has to go to Erik for his kind words and advice on the contents of this book. Needless to say, we have remained great friends ever since and he, along with many other of my friends whom I met whilst living overseas have given me so much encouragement that has helped me in coping with my present condition.

The day we almost lost Chris!

I have placed this portion of my story into a sort of subcategory as I think it is important to note.

Puncak (pronounced Punchak) is a lovely spot approximately a one hour and fort-five minute drive from downtown Jakarta up in the hills, a place we used to visit on a regular basis with friends. Sometimes, there would be three additional families that would join us at a house that was owned by Rema Melati (a famous Indonesian singer) for a total of eight adults and thirteen children. It was a superb retreat and one that I have had the good fortune to reminisce over on our recent trip to Indonesia, whilst dining at the Sari Pan Pacific with a very good friend of mine.

This particular weekend, our regular house had been rented to another group of friends so we settled for a house that was owned by the Canadian Embassy. A bit more upmarket, but still very warm and cozy nonetheless. The house itself was beside a river that would lull you to sleep, along with the help of copious amounts of beer, wine, and whiskey (when our Scottish friends would be with us). It was our first visit to the house and so we were not sure of its exact location, so we drove around gingerly looking for the familiar Canadian flag that should have been proudly flying on the tall mast in the garden. Needless to say, the gardener had forgotten to hoist our magnificent emblem that would have confirmed our arrival, but having said this, the directions provided by the embassy were adequate in able for us to source our weekend away from it all (so much so, it was almost as if this dipstick of a gardener had forgotten to hoist the flag on more than one occasion).

In any event as we had disembarked from our vehicles, I was unloading the beer and the bags and Chris had gone down the side of the house to the water's edge, through some very thick overgrown undergrowth. After approximately two minutes, I heard this bloodcurdling scream come from the water's edge. What on earth could have happened? Who could this have been, as I had not heard such a shrill of panic from any recognizable set of vocal cords prior to this? God only knew!

I dropped everything and ran out of the house, slipping on the polished floor and sliding into the wall; I picked myself up and headed out of the front door and hung a left (this was the only way down to the river's edge as the other side of the building had a residence), as I started to run down the side of the house, Chris was running up toward me, his little face was ashen white. As I came to within five feet of him, he shouted at me, "Don't go down there, Daddy, please, Daddy, you mustn't go down there!" I caught him in my arms and said, "It's okay, my little man, Daddy's got you." He started shaking and crying saying, "Please, Daddy, don't go down there." I promised him I wouldn't and carried him back to the house where I sat him down and asked him what had happened.

He was sweating, I think not just because the house was warm but more because what he has seen had almost scared the living daylights out of him.

I had managed to calm him down so that I could get the full story, and this was what he relayed to me.

He had walked toward the river's edge, which on closer inspection was no wider than six feet and no deeper than two feet (but then, how was he to have known this?) when he felt that he had trodden on something.

He said he had heard a hissing sound and as he had looked back to where he had walked, had seen this large snake ready to attack and it had a large, flat head that had a black diamond on the back of its head. As he relayed this portion of the conversation, I knew exactly what he had been referring to. I asked him if he had seen anything like this before, to which he replied "Yes, Daddy, in school we have a book on deadly snakes and this one looked like a king cobra."

This is in fact what it had been as the gardener (or the dipstick) on hearing Chris's rendition of what had happened had casually commented, "*Oh begitu, pak, kita ada banyak sekali disini pak!*"

This roughly translates into "Oh yes, sir, we have lots of those around here."

What had happened was that Chris was so scared with nowhere to run but back from where he had come in the path of the snake and in a moment of desperation, had grabbed some leaves from a nearby bush and had thrown them at the snake as it was about to strike, therefore confusing it long enough to be able to run past it and head his way up to me.

That night he wanted to sleep with me, and keep crying in his sleep, "Daddy, please don't go down there!" Each time I hugged him and thanked him for being so smart in reacting the way he had done because had the snake bitten him, where would I have taken him to get help? The nearest hospital was in Bogor, approximately a thirty-minute drive away and, I had later found out, was closed on weekends. By the time we had got any help, if in fact if there was any to be found, the chances of him surviving would have been nil.

This was when I had appreciated that the U.S. $1,000 I was paying monthly for Chris to attend the British School had, in fact, paid off handsomely.

To this day, each and every time I see him, I hug him knowing how close I had come to losing him.

It was only two weeks after this (once again in Puncak) that Squibs had been playing with some wild puppy dogs and had been nipped by one that had only broken the skin a little bit but given that rabies was rampant in Indonesia, had been advised by our hotel doctor that she should have a round of rabies shots designed for the fairer-skinned people. My goodness me! This involved my sweet little five-year-old daughter having a needle being forced down the outside of her little finger, just to the side of her tiny little fingernail, almost down to her first joint that left her finger as white and as puffed up due to the amount of insulin that had been pumped into her, looking like a freshly stuffed sausage. It was then that I had had a rather heated conversation with my partner as to how I was willing to take the chance of my little darling of not having contracted the rabies disease than have her be subjected to five more of the finger injections.

Chris Green wrote me wonderful reference, a portion of which I should like to quote here and it reads,

> *Tony brought an "esperit de corps" while working here at the Sari Pan Pacific Hotel and faced some daunting personal challenges that would have laid low a lesser man.*

Sadly, Chris died approximately fifteen years after having written this of lung cancer, but I will never forget his humour and generosity that he accorded my family and will be remembered as one of the best general managers I have ever had the privilege of working for.

I had made some very close friends whilst in Indonesia, one of which was Eamonn Sadler, who I have asked to edit this book for me. Eamonn was a rock, an ex-fireman from the UK who I remember very well for possibly saving my life.

We were playing volleyball one day and I had jumped up to whack the ball back at Chris Green when all of a sudden, I felt myself choking and on all fours, gasping for breath. If it hadn't been for Eamonn's cool and controlling voice saying to me, "It's all right, Tone, just relax," and placing his large hand on my back whilst saying those very comforting words to me, feel I could not be writing this book now.

CHAPTER NINETEEN

Back to Our Home Vancouver

AFTER HAVING A FINAL FAREWELL beer with my good friend Eamonn (who I should point out, once again, has been a great help in editing my book; you will read more about Eamonn in the second book) and Chris, as well as Erik, we departed for the airport in the hotel Volvo, which I used to drive when not bombing around in our Suzuki van. I sat in the front and shed a tear as I was leaving behind one of the best working periods of my life. All those nights of "drunken debauchery" (as Mrs. Green used to call them) at the Pitstop Night Club. I remember I was at the hotel for approximately one week and Chris had gone away for three days and left me in charge of the hotel. I had noticed that there were a lot of prostitutes that would frequent the nightclub and "Mr. Innocent" here decided to (much to the disgust of the club manager) rid the club of this "riff raff," only to have the revenue drop by half. When Chris got back he almost had a coronary and explained to me that it was because of these "ladies of the night" that we were by far the busiest nightclub in Jakarta!

Well it was all over now, along with the free rent as well as food and booze and toilet paper! Can you imagine how much toilet paper my kids used to go through because it was free? We would now have to ration them to four pieces per wipe as opposed to the half a roll Chris Burrows was used to each time he paid a visit. And as for Squibs, anybody would think she was making flags out of the bloody stuff. And as for Dan, I think he may have started selling it off to his buddies at a ridiculous rate!

No, things were going to have to change now that we were back in the real world.

On arriving back in Vancouver, I was jobless and we were homeless. Our friends, Monty and Christine, had very kindly volunteered to put us up until we had found a place of our own. I believe we stayed with them for approximately six weeks before we purchased our house that the kids still live in, with the almost $70,000 that we had managed to save whilst living abroad for the last five years.

Whilst in Jakarta, I had put some feelers out as it came to employment and had heard that Hotel Vancouver was looking for a director of food and beverage, and so I sent a copy of my resume to the GM as well as the director of human resources. Within ten days, I had found employment and so things were starting to look up. Or were they?

I found it particularly hard settling back into the workplace after having been overseas for the past five years, specifically when it came down to computer literacy. I didn't even know how to use e-mail let alone Word or Excel, so was placed on a two-day crash course on all three and must admit picked it up pretty quick. Not only this though, but I had some fierce competition from a couple of managers who had been passed up for the position. They would pounce on every error I made and generally made life very difficult for me.

Whilst at Hotel Vancouver, I had overseen some extensive renovations and had embarked on a project that required us to open up a Californian style restaurant that had the executive chef, the restaurant manager, and myself spending a week in San Francisco training at one of this city's finest restaurants, the owner of which was well in with the big wigs of the city and had us meeting the mayor of this vibrant city along with "Mr. Sunshine" himself (George

Hamilton) and the director of the movie *The Godfather*, Francis Copolla.

Mr. Copolla had his own winery that featured some excellent reds and he had his own brand of cigars that I thought were not so grand but was I going to say something as I sat there at the Copolla winery with two of the world's most famous men?

The restaurant has opened and was called 900 West.

I had lasted three and a half years at this magnificent hotel before being fired, the reason for which is as follows.

Since coming back from Jakarta I had missed the lifestyle and so would get grief from my partner (now of fifteen years) if I had stayed behind at work for a drink and was getting sick of the constant nagging. Then there was this special "troubled" teen friend of hers that was always hanging around and had me (as well as most of the neighbors) scratching our heads thinking that there seemed to be more to this relationship than met the eye.

We had started marriage counselling and when the topic of this "relationship" had come up, my goodness me, she almost flipped.

One evening I had come home from work and had found them cuddled up on the couch together; as my partner had got up to go to the washroom, I had said to this young woman (as I had been instructed to by our counsellor), "Okay, I think it's time for you to go now," and she left. Well, when my partner had come out of the washroom and asked where her friend was and I told her that based on the advice of the counsellor, I had asked that she go home; she came at me as if a mother bear was protecting her cub.

Needless to say, the counselling sessions came to an abrupt end, except of course, for the last one that I attended where the counsellor had determined that my partner had beaten the biggest challenge of her life, that being death itself (as a result of the cancer), and didn't see the need for a man any longer.

One morning, my partner had decided I was moving out. What could I do? I was causing her too much stress and did I want the responsibility of her cancer returning? I called my dad to let him know what was transpiring, and he had said that it might not be a bad thing as the situation was not improving and the atmosphere was pretty tense. After having got off the phone, my partner started on me again accusing my Dad of suggesting something that I should do in order to "fix her." At this point, I had convinced myself that we had in fact reached the point of no return and that my dad had made a good suggestion and that it would be better for the kids, so I had no choice but to move out, thus relinquishing the right to my home. My Dad had advised me not to "touch her" and had to admit the thought of it was becoming more and more attractive as the barrage of insults on myself, but more so on my family, were becoming almost too much to handle.

I said to her that it was she who would to tell the children as it was she who wanted me out. So the next day we sat with the children. She had briefed Chris as he sat beside her as she broke the news, he smiled somewhat uncomfortably whereas Squibs and Daniel just burst into floods of tears that actually got me going, but she sat there as stern-faced with a look of determination. She had said to me that she was digging her heels in as it pertained to this issue and nothing was going to change her mind. I said, "Not even for the sake of the children" To which she chuckled and spat back at me, "Not even!" and she then smiled at me.

So having moved out to an apartment of my own (which *she* decided I would move into) became very lonely, as I was missing my children so desperately and bitter and so my work was affected. To add insult to injury, she was spreading word among our friends and my coworkers that I was drinking heavily (which given my circumstances would not have seemed appropriate, but was not the case) and so I lost my job.

I kind of hung around my apartment, sleeping most days, just waiting for something. For what, I wasn't sure, maybe for someone to offer me a job, but what was the point of this as I probably would not be hireable given that I had been fired from one of Vancouver's most prestigious hotels, and having been the president of Vancouver's food and beverage director's association, word would soon travel fast and so it seemed as if I was doomed to fester. My partner wanted to come up and see my apartment so many times but told her, repeatedly that she wasn't welcome.

I had decided that the only productive action would be to file for divorce which kind of took her by surprise.

After this came my first Christmas alone and I was dreading it. My Mum and Dad were concerned for me as Christmas had always been a special part of us as a family and so decided to come out and pay me a visit. I had tried to convince them that I was going to be fine, but they insisted on coming. I would have been fine but having them there with me gave me such a boost—I will never forget it!

In January, I went to see a lawyer who had been recommended to me who specialized in divorces as my original lawyer seemed to favor women in issues such as this. His name was Bill and later in the year had found out, through our e-mails that he was going through the same thing and that he had wanted to talk but the distance between us was so great, it would have been impossible. He sounded so desperate and I felt so bad for him but what could I do?

In February of that year, I had sent my resume to a friend, Alan, who was working at the Mandarin Hotel in Jakarta, as director of food and beverage, who in turn, passed it to the Executive Chef Ben (who I had also befriended whilst in Jakarta); who, in turn, placed it onto the desk of the GM of Le Meridien Hotel in Jakarta.

It was March 15 when I got a call from this GM for a telephone interview. He wanted me to fly to Toronto so that the GM of the hotel there could interview me in person as this was the closest Meridien hotel and as it happened, was Le Meridien King Edward, the very same hotel that we had opened some sixteen years earlier.

I thought this was good omen, and what was even better was that the GM of the Meridien in Jakarta had tried calling the GM at Hotel Vancouver and kept getting his voicemail and didn't believe in leaving messages, so he never got to speak to him. *Yes,* I had thought to myself, *somebody up there likes me after all.*

On April 5, I was on my way to the airport after having a very tearful farewell at Richard and Madeline's place (friends of ours who lived just around the corner), so painful in fact that my partner had to literally pry Daniel away from my leg as I was leaving the house. He was only five years old at the time and I sobbed all the way to the airport vowing to my friend Richard that I would never ever forgive my partner for ripping my family apart, as she had done.

And to this day, I have only just been able to shake her hand this last Christmas and I think this was for the benefit of my kids, almost certainly not for mine or hers.

I am not sure if I will ever be able to forgive her completely, but am making every effort to be congenial, even if only for the sake of the children, whom I adore so much so that if all of them ever needed any blood and I only had one drop left to spare my life, I would gladly split it three ways if I thought it would make a difference.

CHAPTER TWENTY

Southeast Asia (Part 2)

I **BOARDED A CATHAY PACIFIC** flight to Hong Kong that took fourteen hours and changed for a flight to Jakarta that took an additional five hours. All I could think about for the entire journey was that was I doing the right thing and would my kids ever forgive me for leaving them? I consoled myself by justifying my leaving by admitting that I had had to find work and this was the only opportunity that I had been able to come up with and given that I had made a promise to their mother that I would be paying $1,500 for their child support payments, couldn't afford to sit around in my apartment waiting for something to happen.

I arrived at Le Meridien Hotel Jakarta at approximately 8:00 p.m. and proceeded to check in, then asked that the bellman to deliver my suitcases to my room. I went to the café and was checking out the buffet when a tall balding chap came up to me and asked me, with a strong French accent, if I was Tony Burrows (did I look that obvious?). I said that I was and he introduced himself as the executive assistant manager and no sooner than had I said "Yes" to his question, had he said to me, "Well, if you have any problems here, you come straight to me and not the GM, okay?"

I thought to myself, *This guy is suffering from a serious dose of "insecurity" syndrome or else he thinks he is in line for the GM's job.* Luckily for me, it was the former as if this guy was going to be my GM, I wasn't sure how long I could have stood working with him.

I went to bed that night dreaming of the time I had just moved into my apartment and had begged my partner to let me come home so that I could be with my children, only in my dream she had said, "Yes."

I soon found out why this EAM was the way he was. He did in fact have a serious dose of the "insecurity syndrome" as I had never seen such a humiliating performance of brown nosing in my entire career, as this French twit was capable of.

The GM was of Swiss origin and was of a "no nonsense" old school background, and seemed to be an okay guy, but looks could certainly be misleading.

The GM had a gorgeous-looking Oriental wife who knew she had these wonderful assets and would flaunt them around the poolside each morning. How did I know this? Because I used to take an early morning swim so as to keep in shape and also to keep an eye on this beauty.

In any event, I had settled in quite well and was missing my kids like no tomorrow, so I had called my partner (who was soon to be my ex) and arranged Cathay Pacific tickets so that my kids could come down to visit me. I had found it quite extraordinary that after all of the aggravation she had caused me, she had somehow come up with the audacity to even suggest that she deserved a trip, with my children, to Jakarta at my expense?

There was no way this was going to happen, which was the reason I had chosen Cathay Pacific as my preferred carrier as they had (until this trip) impressed me with their "Unaccompanied Minors Program," which meant that in all essence, you could leave the children at the airport with a Cathay Pacific ground crew member who would then attach a small sticker to them that stated that they were VIP travelers under the auspicious title of "Unaccompanied Minors," and that they would be cared for, for the duration of the trip by a qualified staff member. (Which according to Chris, they were on the way down but the trip back was a completely different story as they were left unattended at the Cathay Pacific counter for five hours in Hong Kong, whilst waiting for a transfer to an Air Canada flight back to Vancouver.) I find it fascinating that some people are like vultures such as when my partner had found out that as a result of my complaining about the poor treatment my children had received on their homeward bound journey, I had been offered a return ticket for *one* child from Vancouver to Jakarta, and had declined it based on my parental value that you treat all of your children with absolute equality and that on accepting it, would have placed my parental values at risk as who on earth could I have chosen to see, without the others.

I have this expression that I use to describe the love I have for my children and it is as follows:

"I love my children equally, but in so many different ways."

My partner had decided that I should accept the ticket offer, give it to her as she had decided that, "I could do with a break and could trade it in for a ticket to the UK! As you might imagine, this came with so much distain to me that on expressing my opinion on the topic, not an additional word was ever uttered on the subject again.

It must have been approximately six months after embarking on my second tour of Southeast Asia that my so lonesome friend Bill had sent me my divorce certificate. As I looked at it, I couldn't help but wonder if the kids had received those so many emails I had sent during those lonely hours I had spent in the office whilst pouring over the budget. *Probably not,* I had thought to myself as I cluelessly added a zero here and there, and with the same reckless abandon, subtracted a zero here and there.

Who cared? Not me, as I was missing my kids so badly, you could have shoved this budget up your "you know where" along with all your zeros that came along with it as at this stage of the game, I really just didn't care.

As the budget was presented by the GM in front of the regional VP of operations, I had almost resigned myself to the fact this there was no way it was going to fly and so would need to quit my position, shrouded in a mist of humiliation, but it flew so incredibly well, I had, as a result, lost all faith in both the GM as well as the EAM as who in their right mind could have had faith in such a bunch of hogwash.

We were all relieved to hear that both these gentleman were moving on which meant that Dominque would get promoted from the front office manager to EAM and we would then be getting a new GM by the name of Brian Pirie. I was overjoyed at this news as Brian had a great reputation, despite being fairly young, and this is exactly what this hotel needed—good, strong leadership.

I soon found out that Brian was a tough businessman and expected so much more of me than I had ever been able to give any other GM and that it was whilst working with Brian that I had learned so much that he would be preparing me for the future.

Having been at Le Meridien for almost seven months now, I had met a "previous" long staying guest by the name of Honey. Just to clarify what would qualify a long staying guest, these are expats who are placed in a hotel for as long as three months or until such time as they had had the opportunity to have found somewhere suitable to live. Honey, having fallen in love with our hotel, had decided that our buffet was the best in the city, and despite having moved out approximately four months earlier, would come by with her friends or on this occasion, on her own, at least twice per week.

She was a pretty Malaysian lady who was married to a Dutch chap and who had a chest that would have made any fellow trip over his tongue, and she knew it.

After having left our hotel, she and her husband had moved into a luxury apartment building by the name of "Citra Regency."

She had asked me if I had family in Indonesia, to which I replied that I did not but explained that I had recently divorced and had three wonderful children that lived in Vancouver and whom I missed terribly. (I thought that she was trying to chat me up at one point, until she had mentioned that she had a friend of hers that worked in the fitness club in the place she was now residing that I should meet.)

I had gracefully declined explaining that I had recently gone through a very bitter divorce and so wasn't interested in any additional relationships (despite my king-size bed in my hotel suite being far too large for just one person!).

I had later found out that she had been working on a specific female, who like me, had just come out of a long relationship and who, like me, was not looking for any relationship of any kind.

In any event, this lady (Honey) was so insistent and wanted to set us both up on a blind date (something I had never, ever in my life have been interested in and so had never experienced before).

We had arranged to meet at Le Meridien Hotel in The Rendezvous bar and when I saw her, I thought to myself, *Hmm, not bad,* and sat her down and proceeded to bore the pants off her with my questions and my quickly spoken English. In fact, she had hardly understood a word I had said as I had incorrectly assumed she was fluent in English.

After giving her a headache we parted our ways and given that expats had such a bad reputation for their "womanizing" had later been told that had I made a move of any kind toward this young lady that I would have not have stood a chance.

Well there must have been something about me she liked because we have just recently celebrated our fourteenth wedding anniversary. Yes, that strong-willed young lady who was having nothing of my advances, had finally succumbed to my boyish good looks and rakish charm. Enter the love of my life. Ni Morniati (her full name or Morni to her friends) and I were to embark on a tremendously loving relationship (with its ups and downs as there are in any relationship) that would weather the time and storms of living in a total of five countries together and whose love and dedication has been proven beyond doubt, particularly when given my present *condition*.

Not only was she pretty, smart, and a strong-willed lady (who is a woman sixteen years younger than me), she was also very determined in making it in the world and is very well-respected by all she worked with.

After approximately a year, Brian Pirie had suffered the second of a brain condition (I couldn't tell you what it was, but it had him fly back to Australia to see his neurosurgeon who had performed a procedure that had required a portion of his skull to be removed and then placed back).

In any event, I think it was the regional director of operations who had decided that he should go on an R & R and so then we had a new GM by the name of Jean-Louis Ripoche who, I had come to learn, used to be the director of F&B at our hotel approximately six years earlier. *Oops,* I had thought to myself as this could have spelled trouble for me, but in fact have to admit that Jean-Louis showed extreme restraint when dealing with me and pretty much had let me run the show. Something, to this day, is the reason I have the utmost respect for him.

Jean-Louis was with us for an approximate seven months when the government had decided to put the price of gas up, throwing the country into an absolute downward spiral that had the Rupiah devalue itself so drastically, the country was brought to its knees.

This is the chapter that I have started my book with entitled, "The Worst Day of My Life (A True Story as Best as I Can Recall)"

My secondment to Tahiti and Bora Bora

So, as mentioned in my first chapter, after having experienced the worst day in my life, I was off to Tahiti to open up our sister property there. Well, what an experience this was going to be. Apart from the twenty two hours of flight time this being from Singapore to Sydney Australia, and then to New Zealand and then form New Zealand to Papeete, it was going to be a wonderful experience I had arrived in Tahiti, and had made my way to the hotel, to be greeted by the GM and the f & b manager and then to be escorted to my room, that was going to be home for the next three months. It was a beautiful suite that overlooked the huge, natural, salt water pool.

I had a full compliment of staff, which was good although, I could see we were going to have problems with the chef, who was French in his origin but somewhat of a cowboy.

He would walk around the kitchen in a pair of cut-off jeans as well as a t-shirt that had the arms removed the displayed his rather hairy arm pits, that I didn't think had seen a drop of water within the last week, and he was certainly trying to run the f & b operation with his very rambunctious and arrogant attitude.

Without going any further, I, in his impression, was not a welcomed addition to the team. *"Well"*, I had thought to myself *"What a shame as I am here to do a job, and nobody is going to stop me"*

So the next month was an interesting one, as I was constantly being asked by the GM if I thought the chef was going to "make it".

Well, in my opinion, I had my doubts but with only two months to go before the official opening, I didn't think it was the time to start looking for a new chef, so with this in mind, was asked to keep my eye on him.

So a month before the official launch, I was heading back to Jakarta, to check on the operation and also the progress we were making with Pub Tiga Puluh, (our new night club) which was scheduled to open within the next three months.

As I walked into the hotel, I was greeted by a very anxious Michel Noblet (who, as you may remember, was our regional director of ops) who had flown in to meet me, from Singapore, for an update on the property. *"What an honour,"* I had thought to myself, *"when a phone call would have sufficed"* but then had come to realize that this was no ordinary meeting. He wanted a complete run down on how the operation of the entire property was going as "this was a huge opportunity for us as were depending on the successful launch of this property to spring board us, as a company into the French Polynesian region" it was then that I had learned that after Tahiti, I would be going to Bora Bora to assist with the opening of this property.

The meeting lasted for more than two hours. (*"Hence"* I had thought to myself *"The reason for the visit as opposed to the phone call"*)

I felt that given I had been give this wonderful opportunity within the company and that Mr. Noblet had obviously every confidence in me, that as a true professional, I was obliged to give him an honest report of my impression of the performance of the GM down to my favourite team member, the executive chef.

So without further ado, I was back in Tahiti with a full compliment of ex-patriots to assist with the culinary side of things (a total of six executive chefs from within the company) as well as two additional f & b Managers. It was clear to me that Mr. Noblet was leaving nothing to chance, after all, we had two thousand guests invited to the opening which by now, was just a week away, and I must say went off without a hitch and, naturally Mr. Noblet, who in attendance ,was 'as pleased as punch"

The following day I was flown to Bora Bora with my entourage to follow within a month, to do the same thing, this time though, I was only here for a five weeks then it was off back to Jakarta, to finish what I had embarked upon some time earlier that being to open up the new Lebanese restaurant called Al Nafoura and the night club.

Needless to say that I was not the only person who was on hand to evaluate the executive chef as we had six of the finest from within the company, at the property to assist with the official launch and so within a month of this rather auspicious event, the executive chef was given his marching orders.

CHAPTER TWENTY-ONE

Please, Not India!

AFTER HAVING SUCCESSFULLY OPENED LE Meridien Tahiti and then Le Meridien Bora Bora, I had flown to Vancouver to see my kids and then onto the UK with the kids to see my Mum and Dad. We had stayed for two weeks, where I had shared my children with their other grandparents. Whilst they were with their other grandparents, I had received an email from my ex asking that I sign some papers stating that we had separated a year later than we had in order to save on some income taxes she was filing for!

I mean, hadn't she screwed me enough already and now she wanted me to lie to the income revenue so that she could get an extremely healthy rebate back from the government

I had flatly refused to sign anything (and quiet rightly so, my family had agreed). So after a nine hour flight from the UK to Vancouver that had been delayed taking off from London Heathrow Airport by four hours, and having said good-bye to my kids, I rushed to the Cathay Pacific check in counter for my flight to Hong Kong, where my ex-wife was waiting with the papers that I had flatly refused to sign a couple of days earlier.

I was close to missing my flight (thanks to British Airways taking off from London so late) and the check in crew in Vancouver had arranged transportation via a golf cart to the boarding lounge for Cathay, and would this woman leave me alone? Of course not! "There was more chance of a rocking horse having a shit," I had told myself. I had tried to explain that I had no intention of signing anything and that I was late connecting with my flight to Hong Kong and that I had to go now, only to be met with the constant barrage of "Well, you know who is going to suffer right?"

I stared at her and said, "I dare you to mention their names!" To which she stormed off knowing she was not getting a signature screaming at me, "You are going to hear from my lawyer about this."

To this day, I have heard nothing, nor was I likely to as she was clearly determined to cash in on my misfortune again, which was clear violation of the tax laws and she knew it!

Upon arriving in Hong Kong at 11:50 p.m., I had been informed that we were the last commercial flight ever to land or take off from the old airport and were given a small certificate, signed by the captain, commemorating this auspicious event. The next morning, I would not be on the first flight to leave the new Island Airport back to Singapore, but pretty damn close.

Upon arriving in Jakarta once again, I was met by my lovely wife to be, and we had heard that we may have been getting transferred to Bahrain. Unfortunately, we would have to be married if we wanted to live there and so quickly set the ball rolling; I made a call to Dad and my sister to ask if they would come to our wedding that was scheduled for three weeks time (my Mum cannot fly, bless her so unfortunately it was out of the question as to whether or not she was going to be there). A week later this transfer to Bahrain had fallen through and it looked if I was going to the Thai Island of Koh Samui in the capacity of EAM.

The reason we were all being transferred out was because of the value of the Rupiah and the fact that we were still getting paid in U.S. dollars meant that the hotel's payroll had skyrocketed through the roof and could no longer afford us. This incidentally, was fine by me, a promotion as well as a transfer to an island resort that looked absolutely fabulous on the internet. "Yes," I said to myself, "This is as a bit of me."

The following week, approximately five days before our wedding, we were advised that Koh Samui had now fallen through and the only other option was New Delhi, India, or else I would have to leave the company.

My God, what a come down! But what choice did I have? Needless to say Ni was somewhat disappointed (to say the least) and so we had resigned ourselves to the fact that it was either this or back to Vancouver to once again join the ranks of the unemployed.

We were married at an Anglican church (Ni is Christian) and the reception was held in great majestic style at Le Meridien Hotel Jakarta. How I wished my kids had been there on this special day, but sadly they were not.

The day after the wedding, I was off to New Delhi to meet the GM and to have a formal meeting with the EXCOM (short for Executive Committee). I was flying out on my first Air India flight, and what scared me the most about this experience was a question that had popped in my mind whilst sitting halfway between the toilets at the front of the aircraft, as well as those at the middle of the plane. That being, if I could smell the stench of urine and this was the standard of hygiene that was good enough for the crew, then how much attention would they have spent on the mechanical upkeep of the aircraft? A question that stayed in my mind for the duration of the flight (all nine hours and fifteen minutes of it).

I arrived at Indira Ghandi airport and jumped into a taxi and asked that I be taken to Le Meridien, New Delhi. The stench at the airport was one I would never forget and couldn't quite put my finger on it until we had pulled out of the airport entrance road and there before us, chomping down on some rotten sour vegetables that smelt absolutely putrid, were seven white cows that were defecating as they stood and because of the searing heat, I had watched in horror as their feces had actually started to bubble as they had hit the ground.

I had put my handkerchief over my face to avoid vomiting and had asked the taxi driver, "Please close the window," and to turn on the air conditioning, which prompted him to wave his turban-covered head and to gesture with his hand, something that could only have meant that this particular heap of a taxi did not have any such luxury, so we travelled all forty-five minutes with the window open.

I arrived at the hotel, checked in, and went straight to my room, which looked like a three-star dump, and took a shower. The grime that I had washed from my face had left a distinctive brown stain on the facecloth, which then posed the question that surely this had not only come from the ride in from the airport and if fact it had, what would the state of my lungs be in after such a short journey?

The mind boggled as I could see myself explaining this situation to my ever so fussy and almost fastidious wife of just one day.

It was 4:00 p.m. and I had dressed in my suit and went down to the front desk and asked for directions to the GM's office. I proceeded to the back of the house that most definitely had an old antiquated smell about it. I arrived at the GM's office only to be told by "the boy" that he would not be back until tomorrow!

That evening I had dinner in the Indian restaurant by the name of "Pakwan" and was met by the restaurant manager who was a tall stout chap who spoke like an Indian who had spent half of his life in England, whilst chewing on a case of plums. He ordered the staff around with such arrogance and rudeness, almost as if he knew they all needed to work there and that they were his slaves. I had taken an instant dislike to this chap and made a mental note that he would be my first "to-do list." Little did I know that this was the "norm" in this hotel, which then made me wonder about the GM. Was he advocating this type of behavior, or was he powerless to do anything about it?

I would have to wait until the morning to find out.

I woke at 6:00 a.m., had a shower, and went to the café.

"Good morning, Mr. Burrows, how was your dinner in Pakwan restaurant last night?"

What was it with these people? Was there a "wanted" board around the hotel that had my face plastered all over it or what? I hadn't met with anybody yet. Or maybe this is the normal standard when it comes to meeting guest expectation, if it was, it was remarkable.

At 7:30 a.m. I had made my way to the executive offices, only to find them still in darkness with not a soul to be found anywhere, so I thought to myself, *Let's go for wander around the hotel and check out the place.* On returning to the offices at 8:00 a.m., I was astonished to find not one person within them. I looked at my watch that said Tuesday the seventeenth so it was not a Saturday or a Sunday, so was it a public holiday or not?

I went to the front desk and asked if anybody knew what time the GM normally came to work and the pompous, arrogant FOM (front office manager) said to me, again with what seemed like a case of plums in his mouth, "Who may I ask is looking for him?" To which I replied, "I have an appointment with him this morning." To which he replied, looking down his nose at me, "And you are, sir?"

It was no good; I was going to have to come clean with this pompous asshole. "My name is Tony Burrows." Well, my goodness me, what change in attitude. He said to me. "Oh. Mr. Burrows, GM doesn't arrive until 9:30 a.m."

Nine thirty, I had whispered to myself, *is this guy some kind of a joke or what?*

No, as it turned out (and when it came to his arrival time) this guy was spot on and arrived at 9:30 a.m.! I was waiting outside his office when he arrived and didn't look too pleased to see me. "Come into my office," he said to me with what seemed to be an even bigger case of plums in his mouth than both of the two gentlemen I had met previously. Obviously, something I was going to have to get used to, these pompous plum consumers.

The GM had made it quite clear that him hiring me for the position had not been his idea but more that of the RDO's (regional director of operations), so I said to him, "Well, if you don't want me here, then what am I doing here?" A bit bold I thought but maybe this is the approach I should be adopting as what I had seen so far had not impressed me in the slightest and so if I didn't get the job, who really gave a shit, not me?

He immediately backed down and with his stupid grin, and said to me that I had an excellent reputation within the company and so he was looking forward to working with me (lying bastard!).

The interview was over in less than thirty minutes (in fact, I was surprised it had lasted that long). We had tentatively agreed on a salary that was twenty percent less that I was earning at the moment and he had taken great offense at my suggesting that I would be speaking to the RDO's about my salary. "Who the hell was this guy thinking he was, some sort special whiz kid?" I could almost hear him saying as I left his office.

Not a mention of a meeting with the rest of the team, not even the suggestion of lunch, so I went to my room, packed my bag, and left for the airport *two days earlier* than had been planned. I got to the Air India desk and said to myself, "Sod, this for a game of soldiers," and checked myself in on a Singapore Airlines flight (and got myself upgraded for free) that was going to cost this asshole of a GM an additional U.S. $450 and flew home in comfort and style, knowing full well that the aircraft I was flying on had nice clean toilets and probably, a maintenance record as long as your arm.

CHAPTER TWENTY-TWO

India Here We Come (Heaven Help Us)!

ON HINDSIGHT, I THINK THIS was the worst mistake I had made in my career as I embarked on this challenge with a less than positive attitude, which was probably the reason I had been fired for the second time in my life.

This had nothing to do with India as I found the country more mystical than I could ever have imagined. No, it was more to do with the hotel and its management style. (Something I was not going to even attempt to change.)

India is a wonderful country with its magnificent monuments, not to mention its colorful people, and its beautiful country side. I can remember one day the GM summoning me to his office over a comment I had made after having just come out of a sales and marketing meeting asking me, "Do you have a problem with India or it is me and this hotel?" To which I carelessly replied, No, it is with this hotel."

To cut a long story short, the manager of the Pakwan restaurant, according to all sources, had a crush on the lady who ran the sales and marketing division and upon hearing this lady say to her team in her morning meeting that "The Taj Hotel is running ninety five percent occupancy as of last night and the Sheraton ninety three percent and we are only at sixty two percent, so what is happening?" It prompted me to say something in my F&B briefing only fifteen minutes later. "Did you know that there are three types of managers in this world?

There are those who make things happen, those who watch things happen, and those who wonder what has happened."

This brought an eruption of laughter out of my team except for one particular chap, who knew about whom I was referring to and who promptly went into the office next to mine (yes, hers) after our briefing was over and had relayed the entire conversation that we had had in the F&B briefing.

The GM added, "And if you have a problem with my director of sales and marketing then you have a problem with me!"

What was I going to say? "Yes I have a problem with the whole bunch of you corrupt bastards."

The next day was a classic as the GM had asked me to present my forecasted figures for the next six months at the next department head meeting (this crafty bastard was trying to trip me up, but little did he know that after having worked with Jean-Louis Ripoche, I had become a bit of a wizard when it came to numbers) and given that I had never received a profit and loss statement for my entire tenure at this property, had put together what I had considered a fairly realistic set of numbers that showed food and beverage figures meal period by meal period (that's breakfast lunch and dinner), outlet by outlet (or restaurant by restaurant) day by day, for the next six months.

So then in the middle of my presentation, the GM asked the most ridiculous question a man in his position could have asked, that being, "Well, yes this is all very good but what assumptions are you using to determine your beverage revenues?" At this point my assistant had raised his hand and said, "It's a percentage of the beverage against the food revenue." The GM looked very confused and said to my assistant in a condescending manner, "Stand up and explain yourself, Sir."

"Well," he said, "if you look at the historical figures, for example, you will see that the beverage revenue for the coffee shop is fifteen percent of the total revenue, and so we take this percentage and apply it to the future months." The F&B team cheered at this, and as my assistant sat down, he looked over at me for approval and got the "well done" wink from me.

He had finally understood the principles of forecasting and had, unknowingly, put the GM to shame.

The next day, the GM came by my office and said to me, "Good presentation yesterday, but next time, if you are going to present something on an overhead projector, make it bigger so that we can all read the numbers!"

"Yes, Sir," was all I could reply

The following day there was a huge storm, one that had the windows of my office shaking as if struggling to stay in place as the wind tried to force them out from the frame. Then all of a sudden, there was a whole bunch of glass that had obviously come from a window above me that had come down smashing onto the tennis courts that were just outside of my office. I thought nothing of it until my phone rung and it was the chief engineer asking that I go to my suite that was located on the fourteenth floor.

On arriving there I saw a window cleaning gondola, with two workers on it, swinging in what must have been gale force winds, hanging for their lives as this thing swung back and forth, almost as far as six feet away from the window, only to come crashing down against the window again.

As it crashed against the our bedroom window, I shouted to the guys that the next chance they had, and before the gondola would break away from its rivets, that they should jump through the completely smashed window, onto our bed. The wind took the gondola for a huge swing outward and as it came smashing against the window frame, one of the guys had managed to jump into the arms of the waiting engineering crew. The second guy had seen this and made his way to the edge of the gondola that made it heavy and lean to one side, but as it came crashing into the window once again, he had decided, prematurely, to jump, only to have misjudged his leap of faith but luckily he had an engineer, who had precariously positioned himself on the edge of the window, grab him and yank him with all his might onto our bed.

After this, the gondola, now lighter without the two workers, had decided to swing out even further and then on any previous gust of wind, came crashing through our lounge window.

The engineers had managed, in the end, to tie a rope around the gondola and secure it to the front door of our suite.

The GM came up to me and said, "This had to happen to you?" Almost as if I had planned it.

That day I had noticed that a Brietling watch had gone missing from one of our bedside tables and I had said to myself, "Good luck with trying to sell that, it's a fake." Ha. (One of Malaysia's finest, nonetheless.)

After having lived in India for almost a year, we had decided to go to the UK for a trip home and laden with gold and diamonds as well as Rupees 500,000 in cash (in India as an expat, you could only send out fifty percent of your salary, the rest you had to spend there and all I could send out on a monthly basis was $1,500 for child support and so had an abundance of cash left over at the end of each month). I had managed to buy some U.S. dollars on the black market but had been advised by our FC (financial controller) that I should curb my enthusiasm as the police were starting to ask questions (which meant they weren't getting sufficient bribe money!).

So I decided to take some Rupees home with me and cash it in at the Barclay's Bank in the high street branch of Bracknell (my Dad was "well in" with the bank manager there as he had used this particular branch for his own business).

In any event, the bank manager wouldn't touch this dosh as he had advised Dad that bringing money out of India was illegal!

I had actually tried to beat the Indian system and could end up doing some jail time as a result. "What a scary thought," I had told myself, but certainly not scary enough to leave it behind. No way, there was almost U.S. $8,000 in value and was I going to leave it? Not a chance as I had worked hard and had put up with too much of the GM shit to part with this amount of money. Now having said this, I have to admit my bum cheeks were vibrating a tad as we went through customs in New Delhi, but I had it stashed everywhere (even in Ni's knickers) so they would have had to have done some serious searching had they wanted to find it all

The highlight of our time in India was the visit of my two best buddies and their wives—Brian and Francoise and Mark and Nikki Jenkins with whom we had a splendid visit to the Taj Mahal.

Oh, and our honeymoon to Goa.

This was quite amusing so I will have to relate it to you. After I think what must have been almost a year in India, I had decided that the love of my life deserved a honeymoon, after all, it was only a very short time after we had tied the knot in Indonesia, that I had whisked her off to India.

To cut a long story short, we had decided that Goa (which incidentally, is a beautiful resort), that had a large Portuguese influence from days gone by, should be the destination. Ni and I had chosen, one morning, to take a walk along the beach and found a whole bunch of fishing nets that seemed to be encrusted with sea shells. Being the curious "souvenir" hunters that we both were, we had decided that we should pick as many as we could and take them back to Delhi as a tribute to our wonderful trip to Goa.

Once getting these shells back to our room, I had noticed that they had started "moving around" as if they had legs. Yes, they were full of hermit crabs. Now Ni, so adamant that these shells were coming back with us, had taken it upon herself to grab a whole bunch of mothballs from the passing housekeeping trolley and then immerse these shells (along with the critters that were inside of them) into a cauldron of hot water, flavoured with these mothballs, for a good thirty minutes.

Not to be outdone by these critters who had shown no signs of giving in to this Indonesian lady, it was two days on our balcony under the searing Goan heat next.

This was when I felt the need for intervention when as people would pass our ground floor balcony, you would hear the comments such as, "Good grief, what is that horrible stink?"

On the flight back, my little sweetheart had decided that these critters, as smelly as they were, were in fact going to be stored in the overhead luggage compartment, three rows ahead of us as there was no room in the compartments above us, in a leaky plastic container!

We laughed so much as the two unsuspecting Indian ladies looked at each other, in absolute disgust, as the dripping shells would cascade their smelly juices between the two of them, each suspecting that the other had not showered earlier.

And there was the time when the executive chef and I went to Beirut and then onto Bahrain and Abu Dhabi. I loved this trip as the chef (another arrogant dipstick) had been denied entry into Beirut because he was carrying an Indian passport.

People I met whilst working in India included Sir Richard Branson, CEO of Virgin Airlines. He came to our hotel to celebrate the inaugural Virgin Airlines flight from London to Delhi, and as a publicity stunt, hurled 160 teddy bears that were wearing Virgin Airline parachutes from, the twenty-first floor of the hotel atrium. A great man and with whom I had thoroughly enjoyed discussing business with and his "Screw the orthodox way of doing business" and "Why wear a suit to the office, in fact why go to the office at all, when you can just as easily work from home?"

The second person was Chelsea Clinton. She was in town because of the CHOGM (Commonwealth Heads of Government Meeting) where of course, President Bill Clinton was residing over the entire proceedings; and what a wonderful individual, who had decided to enter our hotel for a "snack" along with her entourage of bodyguards and security personnel, compliments of the American Embassy. Naturally, I was on hand to take her order and when came to taking a photo, I was so amused at the jostling and pushing and shoving that went on between the executive chef, director of sales and marketing, and the GM so as to be the closest to Chelsea; I had felt quite embarrassed for the poor young lady and upon saying good-bye to her, I had apologized for their pathetic actions—she just smiled at me.

So why had I been fired?

Because one magnificent day whilst working at this oasis away from hell, the GM had been entertaining the minister of finance and as he had left his office, I had walked out of mine, almost walking into both chaps (I will save the word gentlemen for my next chapter) not having seen either one of them, whistling my little head off!

Apparently, this is a huge "no-no" in India and so I was called into the office and sent packing. As you might imagine, I was absolutely heartbroken at these events—*not*! And so there ended my perambulation of India.

CHAPTER TWENTY-THREE

Fiji Here We Come

HAVING LEFT INDIA WITH A bitter flavor in my mouth, I had decided to head home or to base, that being Mum and Dad's place. I had been in touch with a few head-hunters within the UK and at one point, had been flown to Abu Dhabi for an interview for a hotel as the director of food and beverage, but declined the offer as a result of the accommodation they were prepared to give us. Fussy you may say, yes, but I was married and so my priorities had changed in terms of where and in what I would be willing to settle.

So we waited and waited and waited for what seemed like an eternity, for what I had considered would be the right "fit" for us both. When I say us, naturally, I meant me but it was time to think about my wife and her aspirations.

I had received a call from a head-hunter within the UK asking if I would be interested in working in Fiji. "Sure," I said, "for which company?"

"The Shangri-La, as the director of food and beverage," was the response. To which I replied, "When do I start?"

There was no formal interview, just a chat with the head-hunter and that was it, and we were off to the races.

We flew from London Heathrow Airport to Los Angeles then connected to a flight to Nadi (pronounced Nandi)—a long flight but the journey was worth it. As we disembarked from the plane, we were greeted by the smell of hibiscus and were presented with lays (these are the Polynesian style necklaces that are made of white or pink flowers and are a great welcome symbol) as well as a group of Fijian men, dressed in the typical Polynesian style of dress with grass skirts, a woven hat made out of palm leaves, all playing guitars and what was a warm welcome song. It was quite special and very well done.

There was a new white Mercedes waiting to pick us up. As we sat in the car, the driver had put his hand into the glove compartment that was between him and the passenger's seat, where he had stored two almost frozen hand towels, lightly scented with a natural hibiscus extract (that was a non-allergic fragrance) that he placed on a small silver platter and passed to us. "What service," I had said to Ni. The towels had hit the spot as the airport lounge was in an open part of the airport, which meant no air conditioning.

After a forty-minute ride to a place called Sigatoka (pronounced Singatoka) we had arrived at our destination, where the entire front office staff, along with an approximate addition of twenty F&B personnel had gathered to greet us with what was an amazing group of talented singers that sang the Fijian welcome song and placed lays around our necks, something, again, we found so welcoming.

This place Fiji can only be described as "paradise" as it was with the constant crashing of the waves against the volcanic lava that surrounded the actual island and the tropical air that made it so.

I will never forget the house that we had been allotted. It was on a hill along with all the other expats that was nicknamed by the locals as Hollywood Hills and it was a nice three-bedroom cottage that had been upgraded by the former F&B director so that it had an enclosed ceiling that allowed for air conditioning.

We would wake up each and every morning to the constant pounding of the waves and the tweeting of the exotic birds that would visit us each day. Yes, paradise for sure, except for those pesky mosquitoes, which unbeknown to me, would soon have a life changing effect on me.

The GM and the FOM were there to greet us in their hotel standard uniform of beige shorts, a T-shirt that had the Shangri-La logo neatly printed on top left portion of the front of the shirt as well as a nice smaller version on the left portion of the short-sleeved shirt, white socks, and a smart pair of very comfortable, casual shoes.

I immediately looked at Ni as if to say, "We had better do some shopping." I had brought with me some shorts as well as some T-shirts but they were not up to the standard of the gear these guys were wearing. Luckily for us, there was a clothing store within the resort that we as employees of the hotel would receive 50 percent discount (which was very handy as they were extremely overpriced, but then being on an island in the middle of nowhere what could you expect?). Imported produce was going to be expensive, which I believe reflected in the salary we were getting paid.

I started work the next day and sat down with GM, whom I had liked since day one, and proceeded to go through the budget and the marketing plan, as it related to the food and beverage division.

Some thing was cool about this GM; I think that because he had been with the company for so long, almost twenty years, that he had this air of confidence about him. I was choked to find out that he would be gone from our property within a month, and that his replacement was going to be a first timer (the worst). He had a strong F&B background and according to the outgoing GM was full of "piss and vinegar" which means he was full of great ideas and with all the best intentions, but seldom knew how to execute them, but would lean on whoever in order to get things done.

Great, I thought, *this was all I needed!*

A month had passed and the outgoing GM and I were getting along famously, and I was going to miss him.

When the new GM arrived, I didn't like him at all. He was big and fat and would perspire profusely. When he spoke, it was as if we all had to laugh at his jokes, and most people did, except me! I could tell it was starting to annoy him as one day he had asked that we go for a beer and after he had consumed approximately six and whilst I was still nursing my first, he had said to me, "You don't like me do you?" To which I replied, "Do you know what it is not about like but more about respect." He had started to slur his words, when he said once again, "You see, you don't like me." After this, I got out of my chair, wished him a good night and headed home.

We were invited to the welcome/farewell ceremony that involved us all sitting on a straw mat and then consuming "Cava." This is a local brew made of ground "Cava" root and water that would be strained through, what looked like the Kalevu's (or local chief's) dirty old sock, into a wooden bowl that looked like an upturned turtle shell and then would be stirred with such loving grace, much like a chef stirring his sauce before ladling it over a beautiful piece of roasted game, poured into a hollowed out coconut shell, then served to whomever was in the ceremonial party. As you would consume this horrendous mixture, in one go, the chief would chant something in Fijian then on consuming the mixture, he would clap his hands three times and you would be expected to toss the cup to the chief so that he could catch it with ease.

This Cava drink was brutal as after the first shot or "go" your lips would turn numb as if you had spent the last half an hour in the dentist chair; after a second shot (which would be the normal situation in a ceremony such as this), you would start slurring your words and after the third shot (rumour had it as I had never made it past the second shot) you would start to hallucinate.

So many of my staff would come to work with eyeballs so glazed you could tell they had been at the Cava. The only problem I had with this Cava was that when the entire village were celebrating, they would get so high and would start hallucinating that they would forget who their partner was or what he or she looked like and so they (the men and the women) would end up sleeping with whoever looked the best, and so sexual promiscuity was fairly rampant along which came the STDs.

I will never forget the first medical exam that my division underwent—the results were catastrophic for me as forty five percent of my team had to be away from work for at least ten days or at least until the penicillin had done its job!

So the new GM settled in and proceeded to clean house. First it was the DSM (director of sales and marketing), then he wanted to get rid of my assistant (but foolishly I had said no, only to have him stab me in the back later, but I will get to that in a while).

The person who should have gone first was the chief engineer. I have no idea what sort of a hold he had on the GM (they had worked together in Singapore for a while), but this guy was one of the most objectionable individuals I had ever had the misfortune to meet. And it wasn't just with me that he had an issue with, it was the entire team and so that the GM would have a separate morning briefing with him so as to be able to stop the constant bickering. He thought that he was the best thing since sliced bread. Now admittedly, he had a tough job—what with the nine hole golf course and the facility itself needed constant attention, but then, my philosophy on the subject is that if there is a fly in the ointment, then hook it out and get rid of it.

There was something not quite right with his marriage to a Thai lady, who had befriended Ni (until the GM's girlfriend arrived on the scene), and who admitted to stealing U.S. $1,000 from their bank account each month.

A very strange setup. I think either the chief engineer may have had a contact high up within the company or else the position was hard to fill in the beginning as Fiji isn't everybody's cup of tea, particularly if you have a very unhappy and bored wife.

But I had it all figured out! Enter Simba, our Fijian mutt.

In order to keep Ni occupied while I would be spending an estimated fourteen hours per day at work, we had decided to drive to Suva, the capital of Fiji, and check out the local dog pound; there we fell in love with a pooch that was estimated to be three months old. He was roughly washed in cold water and handed to us. We took him and on the drive back, he fell asleep in my lap, whilst I was driving. This was the start of a beautiful relationship. Once home, we had decided that our house that had been provided for us, would need a fence to keep this little critter safe (it was rumored that Fijians were partial to the odd "pooch and chips"), so we hired our maid (Joanne's husband who was a lazy arse by all accounts and who was constantly stoned on Cava) to build a woven fence, out of small tree branches, that would border both sides of our garden (the other side of the backyard had a fifty foot drop so didn't see the need to waste any money on placing a fence there). So in what seemed like no time at all, we had ourselves a very well-built, sturdy fence, complete with a gate for $100.

The first night we let Simba sleep in the utility room, wrapped in a nice warm towel with a clock that I had understood, would represent the heartbeat of his Mum. It would appear that he and his Mum had not had the closest of relationships because as soon as we left him and gone to our bed, he was up walking around the house, and scratching at the bedroom door.

Ni would take him fishing each day and would come home with some of the prettiest looking fish some days. Needless to say, his fur was so shiny as a result of his diet.

Simba would wait outside the house by the gate at 7:00 p.m. onward each night and await my arrival, and the welcome was something quite special. When Ni used to walk me to work each morning, he would want to escort me all the way to the office and on leaving me there, would pull on the leash and look at me and cry as if to say, "Hey, Dad, can I come with you?"

It was after what I would have estimated as being approximately seven months that I had called the kids and asked if they would like a trip to Fiji and got a resounding "Would we ever?"

I had borrowed the a fare from my Dad (I didn't have the $6,000 it was going to cost, handy at that particular time, mostly due to the "gold digger" of an ex-wife, whose constant barraging for more money had me sending all the spare money that I had back to Canada).

They had arrived within a month and we had set about giving them a vacation of a lifetime. We did fishing and scuba diving in the pool. One evening after a nasty storm, the power had gone out on the entire resort and I was so happy to see that miserable git of an engineer, rushing around in the pouring rain. Chris Squibs, Dan and I were rushing around with candles for all the restaurants.

It was a team effort and it went very well.

The chief engineer was not as lucky as all his helpers had buggered off home and had left him holding the baby, so as to speak!

Three weeks had passed and the kids were having great time until the injuries started to happen. Squibs had cut her knee on some coral and needed a tetanus shot in the butt, Chris had gone to remove one of Simba's socks from his mouth and being the possessive pooch that he was, had bitten him on the hand which required a stitch. Then on the day before they were due to go home, I had warned them to take it easy as it would have been nice if they could return to Vancouver with at least one child being unscathed but it was not to be.

Chris, Squibs, and Daniel were playing on a pontoon that was anchored off shore and Chris had pushed Squibs, who then fell and whose knee landed right in middle of Daniel's right eye thus causing it to blacken overnight.

We had tears at the airport as they went through customs, I think for two reasons. Firstly because they had had such a wonderful time and two because we were, once again, saying good-bye to each other and as a family, wouldn't know when we would see each other again. Frankly I was getting sick of these farewells as it was taking toll on me emotionally as well as it was now affecting my performance at work.

Approximately a month after the kids had returned to Vancouver, I had noticed that my team were developing a bit of an attitude toward our GM which only put me in hot soup, because since he was getting lousy service, he assumed the customers were also.

I had decided to sit down with my restaurant managers to find out what the problem was. "We don't like the way he talks to you, or us, Mr. Burrows."

This, I had realized, was a serious and potentially explosive situation because once you had upset a few of the locals, then this distrust and contempt would spread among the villages and could cause some major problems.

This was true of an English missionary whose photograph had been on the pulpit of the church we would attend each Sunday. Rumor had it that when he had really upset the locals with his very arrogant attitude, they had boiled him alive, and then eaten him. (Something, incidentally, that was confirmed by my secretary who had the title of "Andi" or "daughter of the Kalevu" or chief of the local village.)

I can remember reading on the CNN channel, some years later where the immediate family of this particular gentleman had been invited, all expenses paid, down to Fiji, all the way from England no less so that they could apologize for the fact that they had consumed their great granddad—with the hope of being able to rid the village of the "spell" they had imagined were thrust upon them that had been responsible for the bad crop of sugar beet they had experienced since the event.

Well, I had said to Ni, the next time they have a "Lovo" event (this would be when the food that would comprise typically chickens or a whole pig, cooked underground) that I would make sure the GM was in attendance as the thought of biting into his bum, at any given Lovo night, was enough to turn my stomach.

That particular afternoon, we had a VIP group checking in (some personal friends of the GM) and the staff has decided to turn on him and so went on a bit of a go slow, and we had thirteen VIP fruit baskets that needed delivering to the rooms and my team wanted nothing to do with this whole fiasco, and so had left it all down to me.

I was starting to think this was a personal grudge against me, when after approximately the first seven had been delivered, my team had seen how hard I was working to get these fruit baskets into the rooms on time, and they had decided to help me out, and so six people showed up to assist with the delivery of the last seven.

The perspiration was dripping off me and I was feeling dehydrated and had stood up in order to get a cold bottle of water from the office minibar and that was it.

The next thing I remember was being in the back of this dirty old delivery van, as we had arrived at the local hospital with four of my guys each holding an arm and a leg, being dragged into the "emergency room." I remember Ni arriving soon after as they were laying me onto a very nice, clean gurney. The middle of my back was excruciatingly painful and what was all this blood doing pouring out of my mouth? This was the first sign of my contracting encephalitis, which sounds disgusting, I know (sounds like I had been messing around with one of the local wenches), but in fact was the result of a mosquito bite that would assist me in eventually contracting this present condition that I have been so unfairly afflicted with called Parkinson's disease!

The doctor came by and starting asking Ni some questions and then the GM and the FOM arrived and I can remember thinking,

Well if these two assholes are here, it is obviously not Lovo night tonight.

So here is what had happened. According to the admitting doctor and after speaking to my team, he had concluded that due to the stress and heat of the day, I had suffered a seizure and that as a result of my falling, had bitten a sliver of my tongue that was still attached. Then because I had stopped breathing and was subsequently turning blue as a result, this rather large Fijian room service waiter had thought that in order to get me breathing again, he would thump me in the back.

I was breathing all right but would later find out that he had fractured my seventh vertebrae.

The doctor had advised the GM that I should go to the hospital in Suva for some tests, which confirmed that my seventh vertebrae was fractured and that I should fly to New Zealand to the Ascot Hospital in Auckland for a specialist to check if I needed any spinal surgery. This, as it happened, had turned out quite nicely as my wife Ni had relatives living there, and so we had somewhere to stay outside of the spinal unit.

The first time we had flown to Auckland was for a medical procedure that would have hopefully gotten the "down bellows" to have produced enough seeds to have been able to start a family of our own. Sadly, it was not the case—or was it?

Upon returning home from this particular surgery, it was then that I had got off the couch and turned on CNN and had watched the Twin Towers, in New York, plummet to the ground; it had sickened me to my stomach.

I had started to question the world in terms of what we, as a human race, were trying to do to each other, but sadly, nothing came as an answer.

On visiting with the surgeon, he had determined there was no need for surgery but that I would have to take at least six weeks off work! (This was going to please the GM no end, I had mentioned to Ni). So we flew back to Fiji in business class again, so as to ensure I could lie fairly flat, once we had taken off.

Thank goodness for BUPA who had paid for everything, a most valuable lesson I had learned whilst living in Jakarta.

The GM was not at all happy with the news and as I lay on my back in my house, recuperating, Christmas was coming up and I can distinctively remember him calling me and expressing his deep concern at me not inviting my team to my house for a pre-Christmas service briefing!

I explained to him that I was not in the habit of inviting my staff into my home and in any event was in the middle of recovering from a broken back. He did not accept this as an excuse and expressed his disappointment in my attitude.

This was when my back stabbing assistant showed his true colors as he had partnered with the chief engineer and started a smear campaign against me that was endorsed by the GM.

What a nice bunch of colleagues they had all turned out to be?

The following week we had a budget meeting and as the GM outlined plans to renovate the coffee shop in front of the regional director of operations (something I had not been privy to), I had then decided that this was obviously going to be a one man show (the GMs) and so had decided that it was time for the two of us to part company.

The following evening, I had asked if I could speak with the GM in his office, and as were walking from the Kalevu Restaurant to the main building, he had started making some small talk and was asking me what I had thought of his great idea about renovating the coffee shop. I did not reply and so the remaining walk continued in deathly silence. Once we had reached his office, he proceeded to get a bottle of water out of his fridge (he was the only one on the resort that insisted on drinking out of glass bottled water as he couldn't stand the plastic bottles). He sat there, sweating profusely, with his typically arrogant, superior look on his face and said, "Yes, what is it?" I didn't say a word and just reached inside my pocket and handed him the white envelope that contained a neatly typed letter of resignation.

His face went from the arrogant look to one of absolute thunder as he read my letter. He started screaming at me and called me "a streak of yellow piss" and then proceeded to throw the glass bottle of water at me. Fortunately, his aim was no better than his golf game and it had missed by a mile, and had smashed against the wall behind me. I very quietly and calmly got out of the chair I was sitting in and was walking out of his office when he shouted after me, "I'll make sure you never get a job within this company again." I so desperately wanted to turn toward him and give him my middle finger but had thought the better of it given that he had a fridge full of bottled water, and had he decided to go for a second attempt, may not have been as lucky as I had been the first time and thought it better to keep walking and say nothing.

I had thought about returning to work but had decided that it was now 9:00 p.m. and so thought that I was not going to achieve anything more that night and so went straight home.

The next morning, he was not at the briefing. "What a pathetic streak of yellow piss," I mused and smiled at the same time. And when it had come to my turn to speak, I calmly and very professionally announced that I had handed in my resignation the previous night and, based on the GM's request, would be leaving within a week. The room went a deadly silent and with that, I got up and left the meeting.

On working what I had thought should probably have been my last shift later that day, the GM came up to me whilst I was completing my rounds and said to me, "Look, I meant what I said last night, but if you want to stay for the two weeks you are entitled to, not to have you work out your notice, but more to give you the opportunity to get organized." I said to him, "No thanks, the movers are coming tomorrow and we should be off the island the following day."

We had very hurriedly found Simba a home. Most expats on leaving the island would abandon their pets to fend for themselves, but we had become so attached to our boy that I had said to Ni that if he ever were to stand a chance of survival we needed to find him a home.

Luckily for us, we had befriended the local florist who used to be the Canadian ambassador to New Zealand and who had four pooches of his own. Upon hearing of our dilemma, he had volunteered to take our boy.

So we were all set to go.

And we were off—back to base once again.

CHAPTER TWENTY-FOUR

Out From Thy Frying Pan and Into the Fire!

AFTER HAVING FLOWN FROM FIJI back to the UK via Los Angeles, it was time to head to the grind stone and time to look for more employment. I had pondered the idea of moving back to Canada but upon inquiring as to the situation in the job market, I was discouraged to find that the employment situation hadn't improved that much and so it was probably better to seek employment overseas, which I proceeded to do despite missing my children so desperately. I had started to ask myself if it was ever going to be any easier living apart from them, and I had concluded that it was not but that my hand had been forced by the job situation in Vancouver.

I had met with a head-hunter from a company called Elite Hospitality Employment (or something close to this) and had met with a pretty young lady in the Belgrade Hotel, which was just around the corner from the Hyde Park Hotel in Knightsbridge.

She was offering an EAM position at Le Royal Meridien Hotel in Cairo, Egypt. Dad had very kindly dropped me off at the airport as I journeyed down to this mystical city that had this huge seven hundred and fifty room hotel that sat along the Nile River that I was going to be interviewed for.

I had met with the VP of operations for the Cairo region whose office was in the hotel, who had had the foresight to contact Mr. Noblet, my former regional VP of operations, whilst working in Jakarta, who had given me a glowing reference and had advised this chap to hire me. Also as luck would have it, the GM of the King Eddy Hotel in Toronto, we had left all those years ago for Vancouver, was now the VP of operations for the Sheraton group in Cairo and was a personal friend of my potential new boss at Le Royal Meridien. (Such a small world and getting smaller by the day, it would appear).

I had signed the contract, called home to give the news to my lovely wife and Dad, and then flew back to the UK the following day to gather my belongings and of course, Ni.

Within three days we were off down to the "mystical land of the pharaohs" and had moved into the hotel that would be home until such time as we had secured an apartment with the U.S. $,1,000 live out allowance we had agree to the upon signing of the contract.

What a wonderful place this Cairo had turned out to be. I can remember flying the kids down to see us and taking them to visit the pyramids. We sat close to the main monument and I just stared at them in awe stating to my kids, "And do you know that what we are staring at is possibly over four thousand years old?" To which Chris had replied, "Yep, Dad, and so close to the city as well!"

This was so true as when you stood up at one of the car parks, you could see the huge metropolis of a city just behind these magnificent contributions to the eight wonders of the world left behind by those wondrous architectural pharaohs for all of us to muse and wonder as to how they had made such huge, archaeological constructions, so perfectly square? Something that ceases to amaze me today, along with how Chris had managed not to deck some of the spectators who had got to gather at the poolside to ogle over the new beauty that had graced their land: that being my daughter Squibs, who I must admit, had turned into a voluptuous beauty. My God, where had the time gone when she used to be a scrawny little pint-sized strawberry blonde?

The hotel was huge and was positioned next to and older Meridien Hotel that had five hundred additional rooms that were temporarily closed for renovations. When Le Royal Meridien hotel would reach capacity, we would open up ten of the fifteen floors that had been completely renovated. This meant for a strategic nightmare as we would need to open up room service, often with just a day's notice that would require staffing of the kitchen as well as the waiting side of things. I was fortunate enough to have one of the best managers, as well as executive chefs, I had ever worked with supporting me in room service. In fact, it was Samir who came clean with me as to why we had received the death threat.

In retrospect, I can now understand why, during my interview, I had heard the two interviewees in question, whisper to each other, "And if he can on with the number two, then this would be an added bonus."

My number two! What a slimy piece of shit he was too. I would hire some excellent individuals and had included him in the interview process, only to come to work one day to find out that he had fired them!

"Why?" I had asked.

"They did not fit in here?"

"Why?" I would ask a second time.

"Because they were stealing."

"What were they stealing?" I had questioned him.

"It doesn't matter, Mr. Tony, they have gone okay?"

I could smell a touch of the dictatorship style of management here, you know, the type that had Mubarak (the former leader of Egypt) deposed not too long ago.

On further investigation, I had found out that in this hotel that if you didn't hand over 10 percent of your monthly salary as well as 25 percent of your tips to the Mafia boss (yes, my number two!), you were out on your ear!

This disgusted me as here was I trying to run a division that at that present time had a total of fifteen restaurants and bars, as well as a banquet division that could cater up to four thousand, two hundred and fifty on a very busy night, as well as an additional twelve restaurants that needed to open up within the following year, and this dickhead was firing excellent people, as and when it suited him because he wasn't getting protection money! This, in my mind, was preposterous and had to stop! But how? I was no match for this mafioso, so I decided to go and speak with the hotel manager (an Austrian if I was not mistaken) who shrugged his shoulder on my request for his help in resolving this corrupt issue, and said, "Prove it!"

No luck with this asshole, I had thought to myself. The next stop was obvious, it had to be the VP of ops who himself was an Egyptian and who, if you caught him on a bad day, could literally ruin your career with just a single phone call (something he had threatened me with on having followed the orders of the hotel manager and had replaced the fine dining sous chef with the chef from the Lebanese restaurant. This, I had found out, was as bad as if somebody had called his mother a hooker!

As I walked into his office, my hands were sweating, and there in front of me, sat the hotel manager as well my number two with a grin like that of a hyena that had managed to bring his prey to the ground and was about to consume it while it was still alive. Was this a setup? Time would tell. The VP of ops signalled to me to take a seat in front of him. With this the hotel manager had got to his feet and slid out of the office like the slimy git that he was. This left just three of us. The VP of ops had signalled me to start the conversation. So where was I to start? I looked over at my number two and oh how

I wish I could have wiped that grin off his face, preferably with a shovel.

I chose my words carefully, avoiding at all costs the words "corrupt asshole." I eloquently explained that we were in this business as a team and so it was in our best interest to work together so as to achieve our common goal that being the best hotel in Cairo. The VP liked this and looked at my number two for his version of our hotel's objective.

He had a habit of speaking in a raised voice when being confronted and said, "La," which means "no" in Arabic. He continued, "La! How can we be the best if Mr. Tony is hiring useless employees?" To which I replied, "We, habibi,"—Arabic for my friend, an expression I had used with the utmost of sarcastic intensions—"We hire them and you get to see every employee before they start working here."

To which this rather pathetic individual had the audacity to say, "La! La! I never get to see anyone, Mr. Tony hires them all without my seeing them first." This is when the VP lost it and started shouting in Arabic at my number two. I could see that he had understood his last statement was a blatant lie. And boy did he go after him! He kept gesturing at me and would then face my number two again and blast him further with this guttural language of theirs.

It was a pleasure to watch someone being brought down to size by the only man who could have. He then gestured to the door and my number two departed, banging the door behind him.

The VP said to me, "I have done my best now it's up to you!"

Up to me? I thought myself. *This guy had just slammed the door on his boss (me) and the VP of ops and now it was "up to me?"*

What chance had I got against this arrogant bully? Little or none? I had determined, it was likely the latter.

As I left the office I had passed the hotel manager who had a huge smile on his face and shook his head from side to side whispering a sarcastic, "Tut-tut, rather you than me."

The following week was budget preparation week. I had brought my wife in to assist me in coordinating of the relative material. This was going to be more than U.S. $20,000,000, with so many unknowns, particularly with the new outlets that were to open the following year.

When you start a budget, typically you enter the previous year's numbers onto a spreadsheet and then based on certain assumptions for example, the number of rooms that would be sold by the room division manager, the political state of the country, the competition both inside the hotel as well as other hotels, etc., you would enter a formula, as well as forecasted figures, into the spreadsheet that would hopefully calculate the entire revenue for each outlet, meal period by meal period based on scheduled price increases.

The first thing my wife had asked me was, "Couldn't you have found a secretary with bigger boobs?" It was true, she was a big girl (and didn't she like to show then off also?), but she had come highly recommended by the VP of ops, but what was I to say? "Ah, no thanks, Boss, because I think her 'three penny bits' are too big." On top of this, my assistant was now spreading rumors that I was having an affair with the restaurant manager! (I needed this like a second backside.)

Upon searching my files for the previous year's revenues, I had realized that we were missing the financial statements for the months of February and May, and so I proceeded to go and speak to the assistant FC (financial controller) who as it had turned out was the uncle of my assistant. The plot was starting to thicken and it was not looking as if it was going in my favor, as I had been advised by him that if I didn't have the files, was that this his problem?

I can remember e-mailing my dad, expressing to him my frustration at working at this hotel as the pressure and frustrations were relentless!

I had been to see the hotel manager to ask for some assistance in retrieving some of these files and he had just said he was too busy and he didn't have the time to help! Well thanks for nothing!

Then one day, my assistant had taken the day off (he would normally show up unannounced, you know, as if to keep his finger on the pulse); I had dared to venture into his office and decided to go through his drawers, trying to see if the offending files were there.

Lo and behold, at the bottom of his right drawer were the financial statements for February and May. I quickly photocopied them and had placed them back in his drawer, came out and had just closed his door and had walked into my office then who should show up on his day off, unannounced—my assistant!

He was definitely trying his best to nail me at any expense! I had finished my budget (after several attempts) and had passed a copy for my assistant to review (knowing full well that when it came to revenue reports he didn't know his ass from a hole in the ground) just to be politically correct !

The look of horror on his face as I showed him the final draft was an absolute picture. He had almost said to me, "But where did you get the numbers for February and May?" I could tell that he was not impressed.

The following Monday morning, I had received a call on my cell from Ni, at 9:05 a.m., asking if everything was all right (she would do this pretty much each day) and I had assured her that everything was fine and that I was just about to head into my first budget review with the hotel manager, when the call came through on my cellphone and I will never ever to this day forget how the conversation had gone

It was in a deep Arabic accent and the guy on the other end of the line had simply said, "If you do not leave this country by midnight tonight, you and your wife will die."

The phone then went deadly silent.

I sat back for a while and thought to myself, *Who would pull such a sick joke on me?* Nobody that I could think of.

Then as if perfectly timed, my assistant had walked passed my office, whistling, as if he hadn't a care in the world!

I wanted to confront him but if the threat had come from him then why would he have come into the office in such a good mood, unless he had found someone to call on his behalf!

I wasted no time in calling the Canadian and British embassies advising them of the situation (something we had been advised to do each time we had registered ourselves with them, upon entering each foreign country) and both embassies had come back with the same answer. "Mr. Burrows, our advice to you and your wife would be to take this death threat extremely seriously and leave the country immediately!"

I put down the phone and called Ni explaining the situation and advising her to pack as soon as she could. I had tried to remain calm but there was a sense of panic in my voice. Then something else had hit me, thank goodness my kids had returned to the UK two weeks earlier. Now our trips to the pyramids and Sharm El Sheikh now seemed like a lifetime away.

Ni had called her Indonesian friend, Titi, who has since passed away from the dreaded "C," who came over to help Ni pack. It was panic all around and given that I had no one within the hotel that I felt I could trust. I went down to the security office to explain my plight. In Egypt there were three kinds of police, the military, the regular as well as the tourist division.

I had been very discreet in the way I had conducted myself around the hotel as I did not want to draw attention to the fact I was contemplating a hasty exit from the country, just in case the threat was real and that somebody was serious about "offing" me, then they could potentially strike at any given moment.

My cell phone rang; I looked at the call display. It was the hotel manager, probably calling to ask why I was not in the budget review meeting. "I wonder?" I said to myself, then, quickly got down to the matter at hand.

Ni had arrived at the hotel; she had left Titi at our apartment to continue with the packing. She asked I was okay and I said I was, but was also conscious of the fact that everybody could have been watching me. It was paranoia that was setting in but then who could blame me!

I had signed a statement that had been handwritten and was in Arabic that was roughly translated by the chief of security that had pretty much outlined the day's events and based on the recommendation of the Canadian Embassy, had rushed to the Hilton Hotel where we then purchased two tickets to the UK stopping off in Cyprus, for the same morning, that took off at 12:15 a.m. *Was this going to give us enough time?* I had thought to myself. The message on my cell earlier had been very specific with regards to when we had to leave the country "by midnight."

We arrived back at the hotel to find the hotel manager waiting for me at the lobby. He had what can only be described as look of real concern on his face as he said to me, "Is everything all right?"

"Everything is fine," was my reply. Good grief, we had only been away from the hotel for an hour and a half and *he* had got wind of it already, which meant my assistant knew already.

What the heck, he was going to find out sooner or later so what was the point of caring anymore; I now had the responsibility of getting myself and my wife out of Cairo.

We went back to the apartment to find that Titi had finished the packing, but before leaving, the hotel had arranged with security, to have an escort to the airport.

On arriving at the hotel at 8:00 p.m., I had met our chief of security, whom I was delighted to see. I asked him if he was ready (to leave the hotel was what I had meant) at which point he moved his jacket away from his body to reveal that he had a machine gun, tucked inside. Yes, he was ready for almost anything! This put me into a strange sense of both security as well as insecurity. "Security," knowing that he was well-prepared and "insecurity,' wondering if this entire armory was absolutely necessary.

We arrived at the airport where he kindly hung around until we were in the safe custody of the military police.

We took off at 12:25 a.m. and I was so relieved, I went to the washroom, once the seatbelt sign had been turned off, and had cried.

I didn't care that they had garnished my salary until I had paid off fifty percent of the head-hunter's fee (something that had not been negotiated in the contract, a total of six thousand five hundred US dollars from my pocket), nor did I care that my assistant would be smiling from ear to ear, nor did I care that when the group Meridien had lost the contract to this huge monster of a property that there was no call from head office offering us alternative positions within the company. My wife and I had made it out alive and for this I was so grateful.

As it so happened my assistant was promoted to director of food and beverage until such time as the riots had started in Egypt when he, along with his mafia mob, were all fired.

So who had the telephone threat come from?

It had come from my assistant's brother who resided in Saudi Arabia.

And why did the call not show up on my call display?

Because my assistant's other brother was the CEO of the main cell phone provider and had arranged to have the record of the call deleted that showed in fact two calls all day, one from my wife at 9:05 a.m. and the only other one was at 9:30 a.m. from the hotel manager !

And how did I find all this out?

By staying in touch on Facebook with a couple of managers, who had appreciated my stance when to come to fighting for the rights of the honest people, and for being honest and incorruptible myself.

CHAPTER TWENTY-FIVE

Vancouver, Here We Come, Again!

WE HAD DECIDED THAT THIS would be our last tour of duty as the farewell with kids as they left Cairo was the worst I had ever experienced, and both Ni and I were sick of these tearful farewells and so was determined that they were just not worth the money and the benefits of living overseas and so something had to change.

With this in mind, we had already sorted out an apartment in North Vancouver that we had found online and had asked a friend of ours to kindly take a look at it on our behalf. Who would have thought that I would be sitting here, typing this, as the resident manager of the same building, struggling with this *condition* that seems to be getting worse by the day?

Dad had very kindly picked us up from the airport again and we had decided we would stay a few nights before heading off to Vancouver. The next morning, my Mum had come down from her bedroom, only to find me throwing up into a plastic bowl. I was both scared at reliving the horrors of the night before and also very relieved to have made it out in one piece.

A simple life back in Canada seemed very attractive to me right now, with or without a job. At least I would have my kids close by, which is something I was so looking forward to very much more than living in the same city as my ex.

When we had arrived back into Vancouver, we had stayed at a very nice bed and breakfast whilst we were looking for somewhere to live. We had been to look at the suite that was being offered at Spanish Villa and then decided that for the price, it was small but very quaint, was on the ground level and was only a five-minute drive from where the kids lived. Perfect!

Our furniture had been in storage for a few years now, which had been costing us an arm and a leg. After having left Canada almost some eight years prior to leaving for Indonesia, I had moved all of my personal belongings into a storage unit that was down on Esplanade and upon receiving them after so long, it had almost seemed like Christmas as we went through everything, realizing at the same time that I had been paying these exorbitant storage fees to store a whole bunch of obsolete, no longer attractive, crap!

We moved into our apartment and my lovely wife made the place absolutely spotlessly clean and had made it so comfortable that we were finally able to say that we had settled back into Vancouver.

The job situation had not improved that much, mainly due to the SARS outbreak; and despite all the new experiences I had gathered over the last eight years, could not find anything that suited me and so I spent a glorious (and somewhat expensive) summer and year just searching the newspapers for work and re-establishing my relationship with my kids. It was one of the sunniest years in what had seemed an age and I thoroughly enjoyed the time that would allow my wife to establish herself within her new city and country, while chasing down where we were with her landed immigrant status.

We had applied for this when we were in Fiji and so it had gone from country to country as we had done, and we had finally tracked it down in Sydney, Australia, where it had started out; and so we spent the next six months gathering all the required information and then it was it was in our hands, which meant Ni could now find employment.

As it had happened, a friend of mine who I hired back at the opening of The Pan Pacific Hotel was consulting at a new resort on one of the Gulf Islands and they were looking for an EAM. My friend had passed my resume to the GM who had said that I was not really what she was looking for but not to be beaten by this little setback, and given the fact that I was down to my last five thousand Canadian dollars (from an estimated thirty five thousand Canadian dollars savings that I had come home with), I was getting pretty desperate for money so decided to ask my friend to organize a meeting with the GM and flew myself in a float plane to this island resort!

The interview was one of the best I had ever experienced and so she had told me to expect a call from one of the owners within the next week. I flew back the next day and had prepared myself with all the relative questions I could think of as well as anticipating every potential question I thought I would be asked.

I could hardly believe my luck when, on putting the full stop to the last answer I had anticipated, the call had come through and I could tell it was one of the owners as it was a 1–250 number which meant it was from Victoria (where the owner had resided).

The interview lasted for almost half an hour and the preparation had paid off as the following day, I received a call from the GM asking me to fly back in order to meet the rest of the team. We negotiated a contract and I was, once again, gainfully employed.

After having been at the resort for two months, Ni had been employed by the same GM in the capacity of resort information guide which meant she would have familiarized herself with all the pertinent information as it related to the resort (i.e., number of rooms we had to offer, the room configurations, the number of slips we had on the Marina, etc.) and she did a great job as this also allowed her to improve on her English-speaking skills. It was only a part time position and Ni was getting tired of being alone so I introduced her to our second pooch, whose name was "Bear" (appropriately named because of the size of his head).

We had heard that the owner of this dog had become allergic to fur and so he was up for adoption and knowing full well that on an island that boasted two thousand residents during the winter months of which ninety five percent were retired, his chances of actually lasting longer than a month in the dog pound before being put to sleep, were very slim, so we adopted him and had fallen in love with a great friend.

He would keep Ni feeling safe while I would be spending many hours at work but had the bad habit of running away when we would take him for walks. Ni was convinced one day that she had "cracked it" and while we were walking past our house in what Ni had described was "happy family style jaunt" with Bear walking very well beside Ni and off the leash, when all of a sudden, he was off and no amount of calling him would have him return. He was a cross between a Labrador and a Husky and on one of our unscheduled visits to the vets, had been advised that it was the Husky in him that would have him bolting off out of the blue. In any event, we didn't see him again until the next day when he had decided to grace us with his presence come dinner time. Git!

The year on this island went pretty fast. When I say a year, I would have been quite happy to have stayed longer, but the owners had decided that the resort was not making any money and had decided to change the direction in which we had been steering the ship and so had asked both the GM and myself to accept a three month severance package, and given the both of us had very little say in the matter, had gracefully accepted.

So it was back to the mainland again and into an apartment on 1st Street, which was okay but poor Bear couldn't get used to the highly polished wooden floor and quite often, would attempt to stand, only to have his paws slip from under him. Bless him, he wasn't happy there and nor was I as I had once again joined the ranks of the unemployed, through no fault of my own, and it was starting to get me down.

Then the phone rang!

CHAPTER TWENTY-SIX

It Was San Francisco Time

IT WAS STEVE HALLIDAY ASKING me if I was busy. "Actually, Steve, I am in the process of starting up my own consulting business." Which wasn't a complete lie as Ni and I had discussed this on a number of occasions. "Well how about we become one of your first consulting projects?" I said, "Who's we, Steve?" To which came back the reply, "The Pan Pacific San Francisco!"

What better opportunity than to be able to start a consulting company and being associated with such a hotel chain, and San Francisco! Steve had explained the scope of the job and advised me that I would be on a six month contract and he wanted me there within the next two days.

I was to be "Consulting Director of Food and Beverage and Executive Chef."

Upon arriving at the hotel, I met Steve and the executive committee and was made to feel very welcome. I was informed by the executive housekeeper that my predecessor had been let go due to some drinking issues and the executive chef had decided to join him.

I immediately met with my food and beverage team and then sat down with the FC (financial controller) and went through the budget as well as marketing plan. It all looked good to me and so I started setting about establishing a rapport with my new team and it was quite obvious who the stars were and who was going to be the most challenging to a combination of two EXCOM members (director of food and beverage as well as executive chef) that my team would stay intact and so had decided that after a month, I would sit down with them and complete a performance review so as to give them the opportunity to be able to explain to me their career aspirations.

This, as you might imagine, had gone brilliantly with the stars of my division but there was one guy, the restaurant manager, who had clearly not wanted to be a part of what was now my team.

I been given the full range and had the support of Steve to do what I thought was necessary in order to get this team to function as well as an oiled piece of machinery, and sadly, this gentleman saw no future within the company and so he was let go.

I think the team was impressed with my approach to the job as I wore a white shirt and tie under my crisp chef's jacket along with my pin-striped pants, ready for anything that would come along that would require my performing as an executive chef one minute, to a director of F&B the next.

Steve was "babysitting" the hotel while there was no GM, which meant the executive housekeeper, along with the FC and myself where pretty much running the hotel each week or until such time as Steve could tear himself away from The Pan Pacific Vancouver property and visit us. Then one day Steve made an announcement that made us all very happy, he had found us a GM that we would be happy with and he had Four Season experience.

Please welcome Sileshi Mengiste.

Steve had told me that this new GM was a star within his own right and that I should pay close attention to the way he worked as if I did, then I would learn so much. And once again, Steve was right. Sileshi was a true visionary and spent countless hours leading the sales and marketing team so that we would regain the market share we had lost under the old GM who had been let go at the request of the owners of the hotel. Sileshi's family were in Las Vegas and were going to stay there until he felt it was the right time to bring them down, which meant he had twenty-four hours per day that he could use to focus on the hotel.

He would start his day with a seven kilometer run before showering and arriving at the office in time for the morning walk around. I was always in the kitchen by 6:30 a.m. to monitor the breakfast service and so would often meet Sileshi in the kitchen for a cup of coffee. We would then see each other again at the 8:00 a.m. briefing where we would rib each other about anything that came into our hearts. I remember one particular morning, he was suffering from a cold and was blowing his nose on Kleenex tissues and was throwing then into the waste paper basket next to our director of revenue who was a pretty young lady.

I had commented on what a filthy habit it had been as all his germs would float up from within the paper basket thus infecting the young lady in question. This had the entire team in fits of laughter and I was wondering if maybe I had overstepped the mark by commenting on his habit, but he just laughed and admitted to all in the room that I was absolutely correct and smiled at me with the look of "Don't worry, Burrows, I will get you back for this" (and he always did).

It would be fair to say that Sileshi came a very close second, after Steve, when it came to my admiration of all the GMs I had ever had the honor of working with. Later, upon returning to Vancouver, Sileshi and I would be doing something related to the hotel business, but more of this later.

Sileshi and I both lived in the hotel and the only thing I could fault him for was his desire to go out and eat most nights, when all I would want to do would be to go home to sleep. But this was what Sileshi was all about, finding out what the competition would be up to when it came down to their food and beverage division and staying one step ahead of the competition.

Each month I would fly back to Vancouver to see Ni and the kids, and each month, Ni would fly down to San Francisco, which meant we would see each other every two weeks. One month, I had not seen my kids or Ni, and so the hotel had flown all four of them down to see me. I would be working the entire weekend except for one of the days, where upon we went to the infamous Alcatraz. Chris had mentioned to me that this long weekend had been the best vacation he had ever had after Fiji, and like Fiji, comes up on the odd occasion over our weekly Sunday dinners.

It was approximately three weeks after the kids and Ni had returned to Vancouver that Squib's graduation had come around and it fell on the same night as the GM's annual meeting. I had only mentioned this to the executive housekeeper who, unbeknown to me, had mentioned it to Sileshi and Steve, who together had decided that I should attend this auspicious event.

I was delighted with this news and caught the 4:00 p.m. flight to Vancouver, which had me land at 5:30 p.m. and after clearing customs had jumped into a taxi and had me arrive at the Westin Bayshore Hotel at 7:15 p.m. in time to meet my daughter and wife at the ballroom. What a wonderful event it was, and one that I am so glad I had attended as Squibs had looked so, so beautiful that I was starting to doubt if I was ever going to be able to hold it together on her wedding day! (Not if this *condition* continues with the way it was going, I had reminded myself.)

We left the hotel at 11:00 p.m., took a taxi home, then I was awake the next morning at 5:00 a.m. in order to catch a flight so that I could be in the hotel in San Francisco in time for my 10:00 a.m. F&B meeting. I was fairly tired but had decided that it was worth, and I had enjoyed, every second!

After eight months at this property (I had been on a six-month visa), I was getting questioned as to why I was entering the USA. so frequently and the "vacation to visit friends" excuse was wearing a bit thin. We had planned to open a Japanese restaurant and so the additional Japanese chefs would need the visas that had been allotted to the hotel and as it became a tad uncomfortable at customs each time I would come through, told Steve and Sileshi that sadly, I could no longer risk jail (I was thinking how this would look on my business record as a newly acquired "consultancy company"). They both understood and so I was once again heading back to Vancouver.

While I was in San Francisco, my lovely wife had moved us from the depressing one bedroom apartment on East First Street to an immaculate suite on West Fifth Street that I had yet to see. It was beautiful and had a full "en suite" bathroom with a tub that was big enough for two, as well as a full shower with a toilet that was separate from the bedroom. It was a great place to live but at $1,400 per month, I needed to find work ASAP.

Ni had found a job that was working as a receptionist for an engineering company close by, which had boosted the family income considerably

With this in mind, I had decided to concentrate on developing my company more, not through advertising but more through word of mouth.

One morning, I had noticed Bear was bleeding from the mouth. We took him to a clinic on Seventeenth and Lonsdale only to be advised that he had cancer of the gums, something that shook us to the core and something we had never imagined having to deal with. I was assured that he had plenty of life left in him (or had he?) but that we should keep an eye on him.

Finally I had found a job that was being offered by a local headhunter at the Cascades Hotel and Casino out in Langley. This was a fifty-two kilometer drive to and fro (or an hour's drive to work at 6:00 a.m.) and given it was a casino, thought it would be an additional "string to my bow." I had thoroughly enjoyed working with the lady GM who I had an enormous respect for; her name was Emily Quiring and she had an accounting background and was a sharp as a pin, and on top of all this, I think she and I shared the same vision in terms of which direction the hotel should go.

Unfortunately, after six months the owners had decided that the $78,000 I was being paid could no longer be justified as the revenues were not there. I came home thankful that Ni was still in her $36,000 per year job, only to be told that she too had been laid off due to a downturn in business volumes! In essence, we had gone from a family earning $114,000 per year to a big fat zero, in just a week. A bit of a shock to the system, I think one would agree?

So what now? It was getting so that I should think more seriously about this consultancy lark and so sat down and put a business plan together along with some revenue projections that seemed realistic enough, when I had received a call asking if I was interested at all in working on Vancouver Island. It was a small resort and had been open for three years but the owner could be rather difficult at times. I can remember thinking to myself, *This couldn't be any worse than India or Fiji or even Cairo?* How wrong I was!

I had moved over to the Island first and had stayed in a small, quaint little cabin that was positioned along the water's edge. Ni had packed all of our belongings and had arranged to have them moved via a professional mover to Vancouver Island (yes, among these belongings was a dog named Bear).

We had found a very nice house to rent thanks to one of my staff at work, however, hadn't realized how expensive this whole undertaking was going to be, particularly when it came to heating the place. Our small apartment would only cost an approximate thirty dollars a month in hydro, which is a drop in the bucket when between the two of you, you are taking home on average, a good $6,500 per month. I was now getting paid a little more than half of what I was earning at the casino and each time the kids came over to see us (on average twice per month), the ferry journeys alone would cost us $125 per visit and then with the food and milk and the likes, plus an additional $275 for heat! Needless to say, we were not saving a cent and so the credit cards were taking a hammering. Ni was working at a ladies clothing store that was downtown Victoria, which was a pain for her to travel to as our house was in a place called Deep Cove and was situated so far from the main road that it used to take her forty-five minutes to walk to the bus stop, with an additional fifty minutes journey to where she would work.

The situation was not ideal and work was becoming an almost impossibility. Having been there for almost four weeks, I had come to find out that within the last three years that this resort had been open, I was manager number twenty-eight to have been employed by this tyrant of an owner. And he was a tyrant! For the first three months he was almost like a best buddy and yet, on having successfully completed my probationary period, had turned into the nastiest, most vindictive individual I have ever come across. I couldn't believe an individual could turn like a glass of milk so sour, in such a short amount of time.

I had no choice but to grin and bear it. Now I fully understood why the chef had admitted to me that he was an alcoholic as a result of the continuous and relentless character assassination that he would be forced to undertake each day at work. "Remarkable," I had said to Ni, "that this chef was still working for this chap, and hadn't contemplated suicide." Or had he?

The house we lived in was such that as you entered through the front door, there was a guest's bedroom on the right hand side and then a good fifteen steps up to the living area. This was fine for Ni and myself but I had started to notice Bear was now having problems negotiating this flight and it was clear his back legs were starting to give way. I could hear him grimace as he would take each step. The poor fellow was having a tough time of it. Bless him!

I had noticed that he had developed some large lumps on his back and the struggle to get not only up, but down the stairs, was becoming increasingly hard for "our boy." We had decided to take him to the vet that was a good thirty minute drive from home.

I was suspecting the worst in terms of the outcome of this visit but hadn't let on to Ni as she had become so close to this dear, now, much older friend of ours. As we helped him into the car, I assisted him with his back legs when all of a sudden he yelped. He looked at me as if to say, "It's okay, Dad, I know you didn't mean it." I had unknowingly almost dislocated his right back leg according to the vet, who had examined him at his practice on our arrival there. He looked at Bear and had determined that the lumps on his back were secondary forms of cancer and that he didn't have long to live. "So what now?" I had said to the vet. "Well, Mr. Burrows, as sad and as drastic as it may sound, I think the kindest thing you can do to this old friend of yours is to put him to sleep."

That crushing word "sleep" had a meaning of its own when it came to your own animal. I said to the vet that my wife would want to see him one last time before we euthanized him and he very kindly said, "Take your time, Mr. Burrows."

I took him out to see Ni who was crying as she saw him limping, as he so bravely put one back leg in front of the other. All I could say was, "Darling, you have to say good-bye to our dear friend as the vet thinks it would not be fair to take him home whilst he is in as much pain as he is, and the vet doesn't think he has much longer to live."

With this, she hugged him and simply said, "I love you, Bear, and promise I will never forget you." She kissed him on his nose and then walked outside.

I signalled to the assistant vet that we were ready, and she motioned for me to follow her into a room. The room was very small and had what seemed like a freshly laundered towel that Bear had automatically lain down as if resigning himself of the outcome of the next time he would see the vet. The vet had entered the room with a large syringe full of clear liquid; he then proceeded to explain to me that the syringe contained a mixture of two chemicals, one that would put Bear into a deep sleep and the other would put him into cardiac arrest.

I had started to question myself as to the actions I was about to take when the vet very kindly said, "Mr. Burrows, you are doing the best for your friend here."

The assistant vet had a large piece of red elasticised rubber that she was going to put around Bear's muzzle, I assumed to protect the vet should Bear decide to fight what was about to happen to him. I said to her, "That won't be necessary," and she proceeded to move toward Bear's muzzle, at which I said to her again, in a somewhat annoyed tone, "Miss, that will not be necessary!"

If I knew Bear for one thing, it was his gentle approach to each and every human being he had ever come into contact with, even if he knew what was about to happen to him.

Almost as if to prove my point and as the vet administered the fatal dose, I had put my face up against Bear's eyes and had kissed him, whispering at the same time, "I love you, fella, and I always will."

As I hugged him I heard him fall into a deep sleep, with the typical sigh of relief and then within a few seconds, whilst still cuddling him, heard him take his last deep breath, and he was gone.

Bless you, my friend, because as I type this with tears streaming down my face, I can say so unconditionally that you brought so much joy into our lives and we frequently talk about you, with so much affection, always with a smile on our faces.

I went out to see Ni who was completely inconsolable. I have never to this day seen my wife sob and sob for hours on end at the loss of our dear friend. I would love to be a fly on the wall when I finally "flip my clogs" and head up to the pearly gates just to see if she cries as much!

So coming back to the job situation. This pig of an owner was so determined to break my spirit, he would insist that I go into the kitchen and give the chef a huge bollocking for not being on the pass the night before. It was during a warm and fuzzy conversation with the chef that he had very nonchalantly advised me that six months ago, he had drank himself into such a drunken stupor that he had almost taken his life, just because of this dipstick and his archaic attitude as it pertained to running a hotel.

Not to dwell too much on this point but this idiot had me questioning my own ability and then on antidepressants and so I was off work for the next three weeks. This, I think, was also what I have since determined was my "midlife crisis." Here I had gone from a completely competent professional into what I had unaffectionately referred to as a broken man. And, as if to add insult to injury, my ex, whilst at mediation meetings, along with her accomplice, Sylvia Courtling, was trying to screw me for more child support money. I could go into so much more detail but you will all have to wait for the uncensored version which will be entitled, "Tony Burrows and What Really Happened" to be published, and will no doubt be worthy of a few lawsuits as people hate the truth and will go to all lengths to clear their names of any wrongdoings! Good luck, you guys!

Thank God I had and continue to have Ni supporting me all the way.

Needless to say, we had both agreed to part company as I no longer wanted to be associated with this egotistical maniac whose wife was an absolute dream to work for and with and certainly did not deserve this idiot for a husband.

Why were they still together? God only knew.

Isn't it funny how money talks? (And he had plenty of it.)

CHAPTER TWENTY-SEVEN

A New String to My Bow (So As to Speak)

SO ONCE AGAIN WE WERE headed back to Vancouver but to a completely different challenge. Whilst in Deep Cove getting over my depression, I had called my head-hunter and told them I was on the lookout for a challenge and was considering doing something completely different.

They had asked if I had ever considered recruiting for the hospitality industry. I said I had (I hadn't given it a thought until he had mentioned it to me) and so the day that we had arrived back in Vancouver (without Bear this time, although we could have had his ashes in an urn for an additional two hundred and fifty dollars, but I could see these people at the vet crematorium scooping up the remains of some—any—pooch placing them into a container and sticking a label on it saying "Bear"). I had the interview with this guy and his business partner and had become an executive recruiter for the hospitality industry while using my own business so that I could invoice them each month.

It was two weeks to the day, that I received a call from my ex telling me that the dog we had adopted a few years ago was not looking too well and would I mind accompanying her to the vet as she thought it was serious. I arrived at the house to find Bruce walking around very sluggishly. We placed him into the car and he lay on the backseat as if wanting to go to sleep. I automatically suspected the worst and on taking him in to see the vet, was not surprised at the vet telling me that he had suffered a stroke and the best thing to do would be to put him to sleep.

Two pooches in two weeks, I had thought to myself, *How unfair was this.*

So I left the vet's office and broke the news to my ex who cried uncontrollably. Once again, I held my boy as the drug was being administered, although this time it took four attempts for the vet to find the vein. I couldn't help but cry as poor Bruce didn't flinch at all each time the needle was inserted and compared to the vet of two weeks earlier, this one had made a mess of it as there was blood everywhere, but Bruce wasn't fazed at all, and it was almost as if he just wanted to get it over with.

It was the same farewell where he had fallen into a deep sleep then took his last breath and that was it.

It was this day that I had promised that enough was enough and that I no longer wanted to be the hero who was going to have to dispose of these poor animals.

My business was named "Hospitality and Beyond Hotels." I can remember having a fight with a chap that sat behind the desk at the "Small Business Start Up Office" at the sea bus terminal in Vancouver over why it couldn't just be named "Hospitality and Beyond" as he had said, "And beyond what?" To which I had replied, "And beyond anything." (There was no need for a specific after beyond as it was just "beyond" and there was no company registered in Canada with this name, so I couldn't see the problem.)

He obviously could see that there was a problem and insisted that it had to be "beyond something." I was running late for an interview so shouted at him, "Hotels!" At which he smiled and said, "There, that wasn't so hard was it now?" I was so close to giving him a shot to the head with my tightly clenched fist, but decided against it otherwise I would have been late for my interview.

This executive recruiting business was operated out of our new home on West 2nd Street; We had come over from the island and were staying at the travel lodge in North Vancouver as we pounded the streets looking for an apartment, and it was the middle of the month and we still had nowhere to live and I, for one, was starting to panic as if we didn't find something soon, it would be too late and we would be lodging at the Travel lodge for an additional month, something that hadn't got me over excited at the thought of.

Ni took it all in her stride and we had secured the rental agreement and we were able to move into this completely renovated suite anytime we wanted at a pro rata rental rate.

I had set up my office and was ready to get started.

I had completed a few hours of training with the main partner (a very aggressive lady) as well as the preferred one of the two (a gentleman and a true one at that) and would be given a few leads to work with until I was established enough to be able to generate some of my own.

The idea behind this recruiting business is that a client contacts you and asks that you find someone to fill a specific position. It could be a GM for a hotel or restaurant or an executive chef for any establishment, practically any position within the hospitality industry. The idea is that with all your personal contacts (of which I had plenty) along with the database that this company paid for on a monthly basis, but was specifically for us to use, you would search potential candidates, contact them, "pitch" them the position having gathered all of the pertinent information from the client, with the view of them meeting up for an interview and the candidate that you have "pitched" the position to is the "perfect fit" and everybody is happy; the company gets paid its commission, of which I would receive a percentage of, and then it would be onto the next project. Sounds easy I know, but sometimes it could take up to a month to find a suitable candidate because not all interviews go as you had wanted them to go and quite often, could have as many as five or six potential candidates for a particular position; and at the same time, could have as many as ten clients knocking on your door looking for staff, so keeping a clear head at all times was essential if you were going to do your job successfully and get paid.

I remember one day I had received a social call from my good friend Sileshi Mengiste (you remember, the GM from San Francisco?). Apparently, after The Pan Pacific San Francisco had been sold by the owners, Sileshi had moved down to Jacksonville in Florida. So we chitchatted for a while and I had explained to him that I was now an executive recruiter and then he asked what our fee was and could I do better for him as we were friends, and the typical banter started where I would say, "But, Sileshi, we are trying to run a business here, and you are asking me for a friend's rate, what are you trying to do, get me fired here?" To which he would reply, "But, Burrows, if I wanted to get you fired, it would be easy, all I would need to would be to place a call into our boss and say that you had verbally abused me over the phone."

"You wouldn't!"

"I could if you don't find me an executive housekeeper, a general manager, as well as two F&B directors and a DOSM." There was a pause over the telephone, and then I said to him, "Are you shitting me?" To which he replied, "No, my friend, now about that rate you were going to offer me." I couldn't believe my ears, this totalled almost five hundred as fifty thousand US dollars worth of salaries that could potentially make the company an estimated eighty two thousand five hundred US dollars based on a commission of fifteen percent (the going rate).

I had called my male boss and we had agreed to bring it down to twelve percent or sixty six thousand US dollars. Still, a nice chunk of change from one client. I had called Sileshi with this new rate and had received his approval to start searching even before he had signed the contract back from him.

My lady boss had called to congratulate me at the same time asking me if I had "horseshoes up my ass per chance?" I think she was complimenting me on the stroke of luck I had just received.

Sileshi had joined a company as VP of operations and so had twelve hotels under his belt and was entrusting me to fill these key positions for him. "What an honor," I had said to Ni. But it wasn't going be easy as our database was pretty much Canadian in its composition, but with the help of my bosses, were able to put a number of good potential candidates in front of him and I believe we had managed to find fits for at least four of the five positions he had asked me to fill.

It was at this point that I had noticed how scruffy my handwriting had become. "Probably because of the rate I was scribbling down the notes whilst taking information down over the phone," I had convinced myself. What else could it possibly be? "Nothing," I had told myself!

After what had seemed like almost two years of recruiting, the company I was with had decided to close its doors, for some very good reasons I felt. Which was too bad as I was starting to establish myself as an accomplished and very capable recruiter.

I had spoken to a dear friend of mine by the name of Christine Stoneman who was by now well-established within her own recruiting company on Vancouver Island and had asked if she needed any help. She very kindly invited me to take a float plane over to meet her partners and the other lady I would be working fairly closely with as I was going to try to penetrate the Vancouver market with their latest project—that being foreign workers. There was the need for a professional approach for this market as the government had realized the need for foreign workers but that it required a company bonded by the government guidelines that would ensure safe passage to and from their homeland as well as competitive salaries.

I had started to put my plans into place and had become increasingly bothered as to the quality of my handwriting. I had compared it to some notes I had taken two years ago and the difference was remarkable. Even my signature was starting to change from the bold, very deliberate strokes of the pen to a somewhat lackadaisical approach. *Strange,* I had thought, *was I getting lazy in my old age or was I getting some sort of arthritis?*

Whatever it was, it wasn't hurting me and in any event, I needed to find some additional work. I can recall thinking how much I would like to participate in some way in the upcoming winter Olympic games and saw an advertisement for security personnel, and on speaking with a few of my friends at BC Place and NASCO (two companies both Ni and I had been working for on a part-time basis), I had found out that this security gig was an excellent opportunity to allow you to qualify as a security guard, obtaining a licence whilst getting paid and paying you very well during the games themselves.

Both Ni and I interviewed for these positions and qualified. As a supervisor, I had to go to specific training that took an entire week but was interesting to say the least. After passing the exam with an eighty five percent grade, I was now a fully pledged security guard and started to take advantage of my newfound qualification by working for a local security company. This had me working at the trailer park at night times, which was fine but I had started to notice how people kept saying "pardon" to me each time I said something. What was happening here, was everybody going deaf before my very eyes?

Both Ni and I worked the 2010 Winter Olympic Games up at Cypress Mountain and thoroughly enjoyed the experience and made some long lasting friends as a result.

I then went on to the G8 summit meeting in Toronto that had me working as a supervisor. This was a lot of fun also and as mentioned, figured it would put an additional "string to my bow."

Little did I know that this additional string to my bow would serve no purpose at all as I was noticing my speech volume was becoming more and more diminished by the day, and my handwriting had reached diabolical proportions in its legibility.

I had decided I should go to see my family doctor about these issues as I had also noticed that my walking style had changed somewhat, almost as if my left leg would not follow the normal stepping motion and would somehow place itself off center when being placed on the ground, and why was I shuffling along like an old man?

My family doctor was an absolute nonbeliever of the term "bedside manner" and quite frankly nor was his receptionist. If only Dr. Quirke was still practicing, this man had delivered both Chris and Squibs and I had so much respect for him. In any event we were stuck with this doctor who, as you will read from my "Journeys," was a class act.

On relating the changes I was experiencing within my body, he seemed noncommittal in offering a diagnosis and after having read so many books on the topic, understood why. He then suggested I go and see a neurologist in order to better understand why my handwriting was the way it was.

"But what about my constant shuffling and my speech?"

To which he replied, "Sorry but I can't help you there!"

"But you are my physician and I thought you were here to offer me advice as well as assistance as it relates to my concerns."

"Which is why I am referring you to Dr. Purves, who really is very good."

What a cop out!

So we went to see Dr. Purves, who I have to admit, is one professional, charming lady, who proceeded to have me do some writing exercises that I seemed to have failed miserably. She had asked me to write my name as clearly as was possible but the letters at the beginning of my name seemed to seam to taper off to a miniscule form, almost to a straight line.

She then took my wrists and starting to turn them around. Then she did the same thing to my legs. It was strange as I could almost feel the resistance in them. She checked my file again and asked when was the last time I had received an MRI scan on my brain to which I had replied that it was probably approximately two years previous. She proceeded to call Lions Gate Hospital and booked me in for an ASAP appointment.

I left her office with an uneasy feeling, thinking that something was worrying her. The following day I had received a call from the hospital confirming my appointment for one week's time. (This was most unusual as I had been told that quite often, there could be a waiting list of up to six months.)

The day after my MRI scan I was called to Dr. Purves's office again, where upon she had asked if I had been to the tropics within the last ten years. I then started to explain that in fact I had worked all over Southeast Asia.

She then proceeded to explain her concerns to me. She had noticed some lesions on my brain as well as the fact that it had shown some swelling that was typical of a brain infection that she had assumed was the reason for my seizures that had started in Fiji. She then asked when the last time I had experienced a seizure. It was in fact approximately a year earlier when we had gone to Richmond to see Ni's uncle.

We had pulled out of the hotel he was staying at when all of a sudden, I had started to convulse and Ni was smart enough to pull up the hand brake and switch off the engine (luckily we were only travelling at the slow speed of ten kilometers per hour) while her uncle grabbed me from behind, ensuring my head was not banging against the car frame.

"And what do you remember?" Dr. Purves had asked me.

"All I remember is the ambulance crew asking me if I was okay as I had just had a seizure." The vigor which with my body shook caused me to involuntarily fracture my sixth vertebrae.

She came clean with me and advised me that she suspected that I had been bitten by a mosquito and had been carrying the "Japanese encephalitis virus" that had caused the swelling in my brain and that should go back to see her in a months' time as she wanted to run some additional tests on my brain and in the meantime, had wanted a Dr. Devonshire, who specialized in the diagnosis of MS, to look at my MRI results. This had me starting to worry now as MS, I had come to understand, could be life threatening.

She could see the concern on my face and then hit with me the statement that was going to change my life forever.

"Mr. Burrows, it would appear that you are showing signs of Parkinson's disease." The delivery of the message was warm, compassionate, and full of empathy. She then went on to explain that the reason for this diagnosis was a combination of the handwriting skills, the diminished volumes within my speech, and the rigidity that I was now showing within my wrists and legs.

We drove home in silence, but from that point onward, I had promised myself that I was going to find out a much as I could about this disease and get on with it. I went to the library the following day and picked up four books that related to the disease and read them from cover to cover, absorbing every fact that I could.

Ni was very supportive and assured me that we were in this together and that I must be strong. I promised her with all my heart that I was going to fight this chronic neurological disorder with all my might.

The following Sunday, when the kids came around for dinner (as they did each Sunday), I had decided to tell them that it looked as if I had Parkinson's disease and hopefully it wasn't PSP (Progressive supranuclear palsy and something that I had researched as a famous British comedian by the name of Dudley Moore, a favorite of mine, had died of). They all hugged me and we shed a tear together and then they promised they would be there for me should I need anything!

I was placed on a medication by the name of Levo/Carb which was designed to assist the brain in the production of dopamine which helps sending signals from the brain, to the parts of the body that require movement.

The pathology of the disease is characterized by the accumulation of a protein called alpha-synuclein into inclusions called Lewy bodies in neurons, and from insufficient formation and activity of dopamine produced in certain neurons within parts of the midbrain. (Wikipedia)

I was reading more and more about this disease and had decided that, if anything was going to get me through this challenging time of my life, it was the positive attitude that I had shown throughout it and on top of this, I had all the support a man could need that included family within the UK as well my adoring wife and the best three friends a Dad could ever ask for in Chris, Squibs, and Dan.

After having spoken to Dr. Devonshire, she has pretty much confirmed that I had Parkinson's disease and my son Chris whose girlfriend Alex, was studying to be a nurse, had come up with a couple of names that I should look onto at the UBC hospital at the movement disorder clinic. This, I had found out, was the place where you were guaranteed the ultimate diagnosis.

I had joined the PSBC (Parkinson Society of British Columbia) where I had learned that to get an appointment with one of the specialists at this hospital could take anywhere from up to a year but then one of the attendees had suggested I call and ask for a cancellation and after having done this, was scheduled to meet Dr. Cresswell.

I had decided to document my thoughts and progress in what I would call "The Journeys" pretty much so that my mum and dad could see the progress I was making and had decided to share them here with you.

CHAPTER TWENTY-EIGHT

The Unadulterated "Journeys"

At this point in my book, I have decided to change my strategy somewhat as The Journeys are a very important part of my travels and keep on going and so, I thought it would be appropriate to publish them separately, if not for the only reason that they would not fit into the same literary category, so please forgive for ending my book here.

I sincerely hope you have enjoyed my book and look forward to sharing with you my second book that is entitled "The Journeys. A positive approach to living with Parkinson's Disease" This book goes on how show a positive approach can make your life so much easier while living with this life-altering (and sometimes shattering) neurological, and as yet, incurable nightmare by the name of Parkinson's disease, and is targeted at those who have just recently been diagnosed with this disease.

Love, and the best warmest regards to you all.

I remain, yours sincerely,

Tony Burrows

The End